THE WISCON CHRONICLES 4

The WisCon Chronicles

VOLUME 4

WisCon Voices

Edited by
Sylvia Kelso

AQUEDUCT PRESS | SEATTLE

Aqueduct Press
PO Box 95787
Seattle WA 99145-2787
www.aqueductpress.com

The WisCon Chronicles, Volume 4
WisCon Voices

Cover design © 2010 by Lynne Lampe
Book design by John D. Barry
Cover and text photos by permission of D Bautista, ML Gardin, K Green, MJ Hardman, I Kaplan, S. Kelso, K Wilham

The text typeface is Cambria, designed by Jelle Bosma with Steve Matteson and Robin Nicholas

ISBN: 978-1-933500-40-9

9 8 7 6 5 4 3 2 1

Printed in the United States of America
by Applied Digital Imaging, Bellingham, WA

CONTENTS

INTRODUCTION

Sylvia Kelso

To be invited to edit the fourth volume of the WisCon Chronicles, back in November of 2008, was a somewhat daunting if flattering challenge. On the one side, redoubtable women had edited the previous three issues, starting with Timmi Duchamp herself, going on to Eileen Gunn and Liz Henry. On the other loomed WisCon proper—a kaleidoscope of activities, interactions, luminaries, notables, and Amazing Annual Events, such as the Tiptree Auction, to name only the most obvious. I was not an annual attendee. I didn't know that many people. Supposing I missed out events, conversations, people that Really Mattered in the final view of WisCon 33?

Gratefully, my pragmatic internal writing team then asserted themselves. So you're not going to see more than a quarter of WisCon personally? Well, neither is anybody else. In fact, WisCon, like most cons and conferences, will be, for most people, whether they realize it or not, largely a virtual event. Even one of those simultaneous matter transfer machines so dear to our sf hearts is not going to get any one person to every event, conversation, panel, reading, paper, party at one and the same time.

OK, I said. Nobody got everything real time, but everyone did experience *A* WisCon. Their own personal WisCon, running over the same four days as everyone else's. Let's gather the records of as many such Cons as we can, and assemble them. There will be places where someone's WisCon fills the hole in someone else's; there will be differing perspectives on the Con as a whole; there may hopefully be differing perspectives on the same event(s). And where other Chronicles have collected the thoughts of notables, along with the papers and panel reports, this time, let's try to find as many reports as possible from "ordinary" attendees—so far as any WisCon attendee is ordinary, that is.

A large number of such extra-ordinary ordinary people answered my call. I had originally intended to sub-title the entire volume "My WisCon," with an ironic side glance at the "My Space," "My Account," "My Documents" usage, and most of the personal WisCon reports are titled "My WisCon," because this is precisely what they are—one person's version of the Con.

And as I hoped, they are widely diverse, not only in what events the writer attended, what he or she saw and felt, but in the writers themselves. There are first-timers and long-termers, there are women and men, there are POC and Whites: there are reports in prose and reports in verse, reports from people who went to panels and reports from those who ran parties, including Elise Matthesen's long term Earring Haiku party, complete with a bouquet of haikus from past events. There's a report set up as an alphabet from Julie Andrews. There are reports that rhapsodize about WisCon 33, and reports that critique it, or indicate that it is not always a coming-home and recognizing-the-tribe experience.

In the volume proper, these personal records appear among what are now traditional Chronicle elements: papers from the academic track, and, of course, panel reports. This year we have two party reports among them, from Elise and from Brittany Flokstra, who ran the Doctor Horrible party. We also have academic meditations on WisCon, as a site of community discourse, in Meg Turville-Heitz' demography, and as a site of feminist practice, in MJ Hardman's paper.

We have somewhat fewer panel transcripts than previously, not least because, in the wake of the Troll incident at WisCon 32, people were much charier of recording panels either in sound or pix. Nor do we have as many overlapping views of the same panel or event as I hoped. We do have a strong representation for POC, from Nisi Shawl's reprise of the Cultural Appropriation Workshop, early on Friday, to the transcript of a post-WisCon net discussion from Julia. We are further privileged to have an exchange of letters between Nisi and her mother June, a first-timer but definitely luminary of WisCon 33.

We also have some fiction, from people who read at WisCon, and in one case, a short story inspired by an actual panel, Bev Friend's very witty and strongly feminist "The Pause that Refreshes." Matching that we have Jennifer Pelland's excerpt from her story "Ghosts of New York" and the "tail," which describes the process of writing the story.

Two notable continuities emerged for me from this mosaic of WisCon 33. First, the strong presence in this volume of POC: as some of the My WisCons make clear, WisCon is still not the optimal rhapsodic experience for POC. But the volume opens and closes with reports from first-timers who are POC, LaShawn Wanak's Friday-only report, and Robin Small-McCarthy's retrospective poem "Before We Remember," which at once returns us to the mundane world and leaves behind a brief, shining shiny vision of what WisCon 33 could be.

The second interesting aspect was the prevalence of media rather than print topics on the academic front. Of the six people who responded to my requests for papers and/or presentations actually given at WisCon, Andrea Hairston, Allison Morris, Zach Welhouse, and Valerie Guyant and Kate Freund all chose film or TV topics. Only Erin Ranft's paper dealt with a printed author. I consider this a significant straw in the wind for the future of both sf and fantasy both, and possibly a signal to Con organizers, that "media fans" as they are often called, or even media cons, are not merely a sub-section of the overall sf community, but may become its future majority.

After considering various thematic constellations, I decided to lay out the volume on a chronological basis, not least because a sequential, chronological frame is how we all do experience WisCon. Hence the volume runs roughly Friday to Monday, with some clusters, such as Nisi and June's letters and Nisi's workshop report, or the cluster of material from the Witches and Wizards' panel, and the cluster by topic around JoSelle Vanderhooft's essay on being (dis)abled, and Sandy Olson's panel report on "Disabling Metaphor." Panel reports, interspersed among My WisCons and papers, also run from Friday to Monday overall. I hope that as we read through this volume, now or later, the various elements will come together to present a shifting, variant, fill-in-the-holes viewpoint, that preserves something we can all recognize as WisCon 33.

Sylvia Kelso lives in North Queensland, works part-time at James Cook University, and has been writing or telling stories for as long as she remembers. She is a contributing editor for *Paradoxa: Studies in World Literary Genres* and recently guest edited a special volume of *Paradoxa* on Ursula K. Le Guin. Her first fantasy novel, *Everran's Bane*, appeared in 2005, and two of her novels have been shortlisted in the Australian Aurealis genre fiction awards.

A Slice of WisCon (or how to do a con in one day)

My WisCon #1

LaShawn M. Wanak

I had never been to a science fiction convention.

It's not like I didn't know they existed. I knew about WindyCon and Duckon and Anime Central, but I didn't go to them because they looked...weird. People walking around in costumes. People who jumped on you if you mentioned you actually liked *Enterprise*. And those were just the cons in Chicago. I vaguely knew about the convention that met in Madison, but that one was full of...well, feminists. I didn't think that it was for me.

Then my family moved to Madison, and WisCon33 was all I heard about from my new friends, who turned out to be (gasp!) feminists. They talked about it so much, and it sounded like so much fun, I thought, well, maybe I should check out. There was one slight problem: I had scheduled vacation in Michigan around WisCon weekend. There was no way I could get out of it. Not by tantrums. Not by sulking. Not by bribing. If I was to go to WisCon, I could only go on one day—that Friday.

So how can someone who has never experienced WisCon do so in one day?

1. **Book readings**

   I decided to jump-start the festivities for me by attending the Geoff Ryman and Ellen Klages readings at Room of One's Own bookstore Thursday night. I had read some of Ryman's works before, but I only knew Klages from her story "In the House of the Seven Librarians." Listening to the both of them was a real treat, and I got to chat with them afterwards. What stuck with me was when Klages told me to feel free to pull her aside and we could talk more about writing over a beer. Sadly, I never got that chance, because, well, I had only one day to attend WisCon.

2. **Fangirl squeeing**

   I got a chance to meet Nisi Shawl after picking up my registration materials for WisCon. Having never met her before, but having read her work, I could only do one thing: go absolute apeshit fangirlish on her. I can't remember what exactly I said, but I'm pretty sure, "I loooooooooove your stories!" and, "U are teh best writer EVAH!!1!" are in there. And the absolute worst thing was that I was doing it in front of her *mother*. Luckily for me, Nisi took it all in stride. In fact, it may have worked in my favor on the following day, but I'll get to that in a bit.

3. **Writer's Workshop**

   This alone was worth paying the full attendance fee. I've been to writer's workshops before, but none where I got a chance to bring my work before a pro writer. Alaya Dawn Johnson was an excellent moderator of our group, leading it Clarion style. I got some valuable criticism on the book I'm currently editing, and the comments I got let me know that I'm going along the right track. Plus, another black fantasy writer. Squee!!

4. **Author Networking**

   And it didn't stop there. I also got to meet N.K. Jemisin and K. Tempest Bradford. In fact, this was the first time where I got to not only meet several black writers, but several black women who wrote fantasy/science fiction. In other words, this was the first time I was truly among peers. I got a chance to listen to Johnson and Jemisin as they gave readings, and they were *good*. It gave me something to aspire to.

5. **Shapenote Singing**

   Because the world does not have enough shapenote singing!

6. **Quiet Room**

   At some point, all the rushing around and the trying to meet as many people as I could really began to drag me down. So I was very appreciative of the "quiet room" they had. Would've been nice to have actual cots, since it's not easy to curl up in a hotel chair, but I was still able to get a quick nap.

7. **Dinner with authors**

   The highlight of WisCon for me was getting a chance to go out to dinner with Nisi Shawl and N.K. Jemisin, along with a bunch of other people. This is the heart of WisCon, not so much the panels or the events, but meeting and talking with people. I learned so much more about the writing business in those couple of hours than I would have in a writing class, or even at the workshop.

8. **Opening Ceremonies**

   Um, actually, I didn't really go to the ceremonies—I only got to see the end. But I did get to see Klages with the tiara, and that was pretty nice.

9. **Babies**

   That's what I really liked about WisCon. Lots of women walking around with babies in slings. At some point, I saw a woman walking *and* nursing her baby at the same time. That's when I thought to myself: these are *my* kind of people.

So that's what I got out of WisCon33. It was only a slice, a tiny slice, but I was surprised at all that I experienced. In fact, I'm going to go out on a limb and say I probably experienced more WisCon than any other attendee did.

Aw, who am I kidding? No, I didn't. Just think of all the parties I missed. All the panels. And that beer with Ellen Klages. I missed it all!

That's okay. I currently have WisCon34 circled in red on next year's calendar. I have beat it into my family that I will <u>not</u> be attending any family function around Memorial Day, because I am going to WisCon. **All** of WisCon, dammit! In fact, I'm going to participate. I'm going to get on panels. I'm going to volunteer. I am going to throw myself headfirst into WisCon. And I plan on having that beer with Klages, even though I pretty much hate the taste of beer. But I bet next year, it's going to taste so sweet.

LaShawn M. Wanak is a Chicago transplant to Madison, WI. She's written speculative fiction for many short story markets, including *Ideomancer* and *The Town Drunk.* Currently, she's editing her first fantasy novel. You can find more about her at http://tbonecafe.wordpress.com.

Glossophilia: Report on the Cultural Appropriation Workshop

Nisi Shawl

On Location

At WisCon 33 I was on one panel that wasn't going to be a panel. *Cultural Appropriation 101* was supposed to be a workshop. At least, that's what the Programming Committee had asked for. But then we only had your normal panel-length time slot of 75 minutes to do it in.

"We" in this case consisted of myself and Victor J. Raymond of the Carl Brandon Society's Steering Committee, plus Cabell Gathman of the University of Wisconsin. We met briefly on Friday for lunch in a restaurant on State Street to discuss our expectations and compare various strategies we'd used individually in the past. We decided to try a little of everything.

At 3:30, in the Assembly Room, the three of us took our seats at a low table under a low ceiling and faced a crowd of chairs. Full chairs. The convention hadn't even officially started, but people wanted to do this thing. They wanted to talk about cultural appropriation and race and the genre, and they wanted to do it right. Geoff Ryman, one of the GoHs, sat with pen poised expectantly—was he waiting to take notes? While Cabell madly scissored through magazines in search of photos for the writing exercise I planned to end the session with, Victor and I made opening remarks and took some questions from workshop participants. One or two people attempted to repurpose the workshop so that it was all and exclusively about *them*. We had been expecting these attempts, and dealt with them using salt, brevity, and reminders that we were here to do something constructive and practical with our time. The project: putting together a glossary of words and phrases useful in talking about cultural diversity.

I used an oversized pad of paper and a green Sharpie to note down audience questions, concerns, comments, and consensus. This gave the project focus; it made our progress manifest while acknowledging the existence of points we had no intention of addressing in depth given our time constraints.

Here are some of the terms we talked about, with definitions:

> ***RACISM:*** A system of advantage based on race. Unfortunately, ***racism*** is not dead.
>
> ***HONORARY WHITENESS***: I first heard of this term from linguistic anthropologist and Carl Brandon Society co-founder MJ Hardman. If a white person likes a person of color and thinks that person of color is righteous and good, and therefore like themselves, they may accord that person of color ***honorary whiteness***. This is usually done unconsciously.
>
> ***PAWS***: A playful term based on the way paws are given out in the course of the children's show "Blue's Clues." Somebody who's extraordinarily clueful about cultural and racial issues has four ***paws***.
>
> ***COOKIE***: A very public reward for behaving commendably in regards to racial or cultural issues. Often, seeking said ***cookie*** is the secret motivation for such behavior. (Note: ***cookies*** are the imaginary, self-bestowed, and parodic equivalent of ***paws***.)
>
> ***CLUEFULNESS***: Of a certain level of empathy and understanding when it comes to the situations of those of a non-dominant cultural background, race, etc. Applied to those of the correspondingly dominant background. Many of my white friends exhibit a high degree of ***cluefulness***.
>
> ***POSEE***: An acronym of my invention, standing for Person of Southern European Extraction. Some ***POSEEs*** argue that they are not white, and historically many have had to struggle to be accepted as white.

> ***PONEE***: My companion acronym, standing for Person of Northern European Extraction. The whitest of the white; John Aegard is my little ***PONEE***
>
> ***THE UNMARKED STATE***: Possessing characteristics seen as "normal," and thus not worth being mentioned. In this society, at this time, this includes being white, male, heterosexual, cisgendered, affluent, and with certain physical abilities. Just about everyone deviates from ***the unmarked state*** in one way or another, though some ways are deemed important and others are not.

After all of everyone's talking, we wound up with only seventeen minutes to do the final exercise. I explained it while Cabell and Victor distributed pairs of photographs, each featuring a single human being. Despite Cabell's best efforts, we were short on materials. So everyone had to share. Which was fine.

The first part of the exercise was to write about differences between the two humans pictured in the photos participants received. The second part was to write about the ways they were the same. As when my co-author Cynthia Ward and I teach this exercise during the Writing the Other workshop, questions arose about the "right" way to do this. I deflected the questions as best I could, aiming participants away from answers, toward the process and the revelations it provoked in them. There wasn't time to share what any of us had written, but I know from past experience that most people have more difficulty picking out similarities than differences. A few tried to turn their results in to me, but I told them those were theirs to keep.

At 4:45 we weren't finished, but we were done. It was time to move on. The chairs emptied fairly quickly, though some people stayed around long enough to buy copies of *Writing the Other* that the Carl Brandon Society was selling as a fundraiser. Among these CBS supporters was Patricia C. Wrede, who had sat in the first row knitting silently throughout the workshop. Wrede was at the center of 2009's second iteration of "Race Fail," aka "Mammoth Fail." Both Fails were online controversies concerned with the fantastic genres' representations of race and culture—or the lack thereof. Wrede told me as I autographed her copy of the book that she'd come to listen rather than speak, that though she objected to some of the ways her work had been characterized, she thought it was more important to hear what others wanted to say than to continually try to restate her own point.

I would love to get additional feedback about Cultural Appropriation 101 and the exercise from anyone who took part.

Offsite

What begins at WisCon doesn't necessarily end there. The truncated workshop that Cabell, Victor, and I put together was intended to provide rhetorical tools for the rest of the weekend. The effort to choose and refine these tools has continued long afterwards.

In June, not quite a month after WisCon 33, K. Tempest Bradford invited me to guest blog for The Angry Black Woman. My post titled "Glossophilia" began with a condensed version of the account above, then asked my readers to keep the glossary project going. I ended that post with:

"Here are a few terms that could use definitions. Try to be smart and nice.

PEOPLE OF COLOR

MAGICAL NEGRO

EXOTICIZING

ESSENTIALISM

And I'm sure there must be others."

I received forty-one comments. I thought that was pretty good. I'm reproducing some of them here.

ESSENTIALISM

Only a couple of comments addressed essentialism. **Momsomniac** described it as "The erroneous but socially accepted belief that one's sex or skin color pre-determines behavior." Elegantly brief.

MAGICAL NEGRO

In contrast to essentialism, the Magical Negro led to a longish discussion, with many examples given. For instance, **Jonquil** concentrated on the transfer of values and knowledge inexplicably absent from characters representing the dominant cultural paradigm, defining the Magical Negro as "the walking embodiment of human values that the (usually) white protagonist seems to lack until they get to know [them]." Her examples were "Bagger Vance" and "The Green Mile."

Vitamin A's definition stuck most closely to my sense of the term: "A trope in literature and popular cultural that stereotypes a secondary black character as unrealistically 'good,' often possessing supernatural or mystical qualities, whose existence inevitably serves the interests of white protagonists." Tying the idea to stories and stressing its connection with the "supernatural or mystical" reflected my own run-ins with it in the fantastic genre.

I then offered my own definition: "A magically powerful yet completely subservient character who dies in the service of a protagonist of the unmarked state," and pointed to Nnedi Okorafor's story "The Magical Negro" in *Dark Matter: Reading the Bones*. I copped to having tried a few times to write a "Magical Honky" story, coming closest with my (at this time unpublished) novella "Something More."

Angie added another important point: the Magical Negro has "no significant goals or interests of his own, but rather prioritizes the goals and interests of the white protagonist."

EXOTICIZING

Though the word exoticizing didn't trigger many more comments than the Magical Negro, attempts at defining it as a term became convoluted. **Jonquil** wrote that it consisted of: "taking a trait of another race or culture and fantasizing about it, then substituting your fantasy (often sexual) for the experienced reality of that trait. The classic example is the Western conception of the harem, which has very little to do with the hareem...."

Loligo noted that exoticizing is "rooted in ambivalence," involving the dominant culture's idealization of an element from a non-dominant culture, "depicting it as beautiful, or charming, or exciting, while simultaneously Othering it by denying its place in normal human experience."

Bindicated thought it important to include "something about how it strips the humanity from the exoticized POC, boiling his/her entire individual nature down to a particular characteristic that the entire race or ethnic group is supposed to share."

Thejudge wrote about exoticizing using the second person voice/viewpoint, which gave her definition a personal and anecdotal feel: "Usually occurs as a result of being miraculously visible in a white world. Suddenly, you are stared at by multiple onlookers wherever you go, and you have to be mixed if they find you attractive. People must touch your skin to see if it is hard. They must touch your hair, or they are shocked that you can grow hair. They wonder if you have bleached your skin, had collagen injections, or cheekbone implants. All because they are now forced to look at someone different."

PEOPLE OF COLOR

This term proved the most difficult to define of the four I asked for help with. One of the first comments on it came with a footnote. **Diatryma** saw a person of color as "someone who identifies* as a member of a group which is not privileged in society for reasons correlated to ancestry…."

> *The footnote for "identifies" explained that though she was willing to define the term, she didn't perceive herself as having permission to decide who it applied to.

Momsomniac further undercut the readiness with which a definition of POC might be applied when questioning whether or not she would so self-define, in light of others' perceptions: "While I am technically of mixed white/indigenous ancestry, it has ONLY occasionally affected how people see me…. Most of the time I am perceived as white." When this isn't the case, "the assumption is almost ALWAYS (inaccurately) that I am Hispanic." While acknowledging that there are "undercover" or "covert" POC (a la Walter White, former head of the NAACP, who posed as a white reporter when covering lynch riots in 1919 Arkansas) and noting that a history of poverty weakened her position of privilege, she thought that because she wasn't subject to the disadvantages most POC face, she might not be justified in saying she was one.

Thejudge conflated the phrases "people of color" and "colored people," writing that POC were those "of partial or mixed African ancestry who reject the term 'black' and absolutely hate to hear the term African American." Several commenters thought they ought to set her straight; **Godheval** called her definition "too exclusive" and opined that other people of non-European ancestry could "find common ground and ideological unity under the banner 'people of color.'" But **Thejudge** rejected this correction. She wrote back that "people with an identifiable ethnicity such as Asians or Latinos are referred to as such," making people of color a euphemistic description for blacks.

During discussions on the Carl Brandon Society list serve I had discovered that "person of color" is a primarily USian term, or at least one used primarily in the Western Hemisphere. As a phrase it was more or less meaningless to European subscribers, so I wasn't surprised that it provoked disagreement.

Original Lee's succinct definition of POC came closest to the way I'm accustomed to using it: "Anyone who is, to the casual observer, not white. Often used in the plural to indicate that one is talking about a group of people not privileged by skin color."

The definitions posted by **Zahra**, a self-described "person of pallor," may have been the wittiest, though the first was certainly the longest: "An umbrella term raised in the face of the rain of colonialism and discrimination. A self-claimed identity that brings together people from the many cultures tired of being spat on by clouds in the shape of European and American hegemonic power. (Said rain may be historic, direct, economic, ongoing, and/or unpredictable.) There are places that claim to sell it, but it can most likely be found in the home you grew up in with other protective gear. Like many umbrellas, it might not be big enough or the right shape, but it requires standing together to use it well." She also included a much shorter companion definition meant just for white people: "Someone who knows more than you do about racism."

Amendments

In addition to coming up with definitions for the four terms I'd asked for help with, some Angry Black Woman readers commented on, challenged, and corrected terms I had presented as defined.

COOKIE

Betty wrote: "I tend to use COOKIE to be the reward not for behaving commendably...but rather...the reward for failing to be a huge asshole: 'I never followed you around the store to see if you stole stuff, where's my cookie!?' COOKIE is...the reward for doing literally the least you could do." That's closer, I think, to majority usage than the definition I originally offered.

HONORARY WHITENESS

I was surprised that this term proved contentious. Not only had I provided a clear definition, I had cited an authority when I did so. Yet commenters sought to apply the term to people and situations I had never before considered pertinent: so-called "model minorities" such as Asians, who are often associated with academic achievement; ante- and post-bellum "house niggers," who conform to white society's expectations of them in as unthreatening a manner as possible; POSEES, Jews, and other ethnic groups denied whiteness in historic times. They also questioned whether it was possible to accord, even temporarily, the privilege inherent in whiteness to a person of color. **Godheval** introduced the idea of "honorary neutrality," a situation in which "race is temporarily not seen by the white person in question—" a highly unstable situation. But as MJ pointed out when I brought this exchange to her attention, neutrality is not an option: "...in our system there IS no 'neutral.' Belonging to a 'race' is obligatory, just as belonging to a 'sex' is, among other things. 'Honorary' is neither permanent nor everywhere; it may be temporary and local."

Thejudge's definition of an "Honorary White" began, "The object of the words, 'When I look at you, I don't see a black person, I see a human being.'" This accorded both with **Godheval's** concept of neutrality and what MJ meant by the original term. Because whiteness is deemed this society's norm, its bestowal is seen as the bestowal of unmarkedness, hence neutrality. As she says, "From the white person it is always believed to be a compliment. It is, of course, racist, profoundly, denying even the possibility of the 'other' having good qualities."

POSEE

One commenter appeared disturbed by my new-minted acronyms. In the original version, my definition of a Person of Southern European Extraction lacked the last clause in the final sentence. **Posee Bitch** reminded us that "race is a cultural construct," with whiteness seen as the norm; anyone denied whiteness by the dominant culture, she wrote, has been "othered" and classified as "not white." "So, the fact that I am asked DAILY what my ethnicity is," she continued, demonstrated her classification as outside the white "norm." Her experience was the converse of **Momsomniac's**, and she seemed to view my definition of POSEE as alternately devaluing and describing it, with corresponding changes in the tone of her post: "... alas, I am according to you, a POSEE. I guess I should just throw out my t-shirt that says, 'of questionable ethnicity' and replace it with one that says, 'POSEE' and therefore answers the question before it's asked, in the way a 'black' woman tells me is OK. Fuck my ancestors and how much closer their island was to Africa than to Europe. Fuck what I actually look like, 'cause this post has identified me. Thank you soooo much. Really. Thanks; I hope this catches on:)"

Bindicated identified herself as another POSEE and wrote that she could sympathize with "members of the black community who feel suspicious of POSEEs who don't self-identify as white," because in the U.S. "most of them have fought hard to be counted as 'white' and do not embrace any connection to Africa, and have benefitted societally from doing so." After further discussion, I added the final sentence's final clause describing the POSEE's historic struggle for whiteness.

And So On....

The project of creating a glossary supportive of discussions of race and cultural appropriation began at WisCon 33. It hasn't ended yet. This essay continues it. My original post on this subject appeared on the Angry Black Woman blog on June 12, 2009. Comments on these terms continued through July 25, 2009. They may resume at any time. Now, if you like.

Nisi Shawl's collection *Filter House* won the 2008 Tiptree Award. She received two World Fantasy Award nominations in 2009, for *Filter House* and her novella "Good Boy." Shawl is co-author of *Writing the Other* and a founding member of the Carl Brandon Society. She serves on the Board of Directors of the Clarion West Writers Workshop, which she attended in 1992.

My WisCon #2

Dear Nisi:

Subject: WisCon Experience

I am writing you to let you know how much I appreciate you inviting me to attend **WisCon**. I thoroughly enjoyed sharing the hotel suite and the entire experience with you. I realized that it has been a long time since just you and I have spent time together, and I consider that a wonderful gift. Let me tell you about how I experienced my first WisCon.

I loved it all. But it is difficult for me to say which part of the convention was the best. There was so much more going on than I ever could have guessed: workshops, panel discussions, vendors, entertainers, games, food et al. The sheer number, about 1,000 people who came from the across the USA and other countries, was overwhelming. Everyone I met knew you, respected your work, and treated you as royalty. The beautiful crown you were given to wear during the convention was an additional honor. I, therefore, became "Mother of Princess Nisi," a role I soon adapted to for the remainder of the weekend.

But seriously, I gained the most insight from the panel discussions where writers discussed their creative processes and also read from their work. I had the most fun in the session where we made our own party hats for the celebration. Undoubtedly, the auction during the general session was the highlight of the events, except of course the Awards Banquet when you were recognized for your book of short stories, *Filter House,* and given the James Tiptree Jr. Award. I will never forget your acknowledgment of me for the role you felt I played in your success.

All this was pretty heady stuff for a first time attendee, but I think that this will just be the beginning. I hope to attend WisCon 34, 35, 36, and many more, with you.

Love,

Mom

June Cotton began her working life in 1950 at the age of fourteen when, an early graduate of Bloomingdale High School, she was hired by Michigan Bell Telephone as a long distance telephone operator. In 1967 she embarked on a career with the Michigan Employment Security Commission, retiring from the position of Deputy Director for 100 branch offices in 1995. While working she attended Western Michigan, Wayne State, and Michigan State Universities, also raising her three daughters (Gina, Julie, and Denise—aka Nisi) practically single-handed. In retirement she is a supporter of the Democratic Party and a frequent volunteer in political campaigns. June also volunteers as Chairperson of the NAACP's Kalamazoo branch of their Labor and Industry Committee. She lives in Kalamazoo, MI, with her youngest daughter, Gina, and three of her four grandchildren. This is her first publication.

Dear Mom:

Re: WisCon Experience

Thank you for writing me about your first WisCon experience. And thank you even more for having it—for attending WisCon 33 with me and being there when I received the Tiptree.

You were the first person I told about being one of this year's two Tiptree Award winners, of course. It was a secret! But I told you. You deserved to know. And, okay, I told a few others. Among them was Jim Frenkel, the Tor editor reading my YA manuscript "Verde," who said, "It doesn't get any better than this. The first award is always the high point." He had no way of knowing how true that was for me. Because he didn't know you, and he didn't know how wonderful you are and how much my writing owes to you, and he certainly didn't know (at the time I told him about the award, neither did I) that you were coming to the convention with me to be present at the ceremony.

You have always been a marvelous, magical person. I've seen pictures of you as a teenager: gawky and adorable, your face shining like the Rose that is your middle name. I remember hiding under your skirts in one of your rare housewifely moments in the kitchen on Park Street, when I was just a toddler. Mostly you were at work, of course. At fourteen you'd lied about your age and hired on as a switchboard operator at Michigan Bell, and you worked there most of my childhood. After the divorce you worked two full-time jobs and went to school. By the time you retired you ran the whole state's unemployment office.

When you weren't working or studying or taking care of me and Julie and Gina, you were picketing drugstores because of their racist hiring policies or going door-to-door to elect liberal politicians. All my friends in school envied me my strong, beautiful mother, a feminist and a forward-thinker who taught me how to look out for myself, then trusted me to use what I had learned. One piece of advice you gave me that I've felt grateful for on numerous occasions: "No white powders."

The extent of your influence on my writing may have come as a surprise to both of us. I was named for my father, and it's his avowed dream I've fulfilled by becoming a professional writer. As I found out last year, you yourself are afraid to write. Still you managed to inspire me. My first and firmest ideal of the feminine is you. You are my mirror, as I am yours. The power of our connection, the psychic link we've always shared, draws me again and again to examine how women relate to one another. That attraction, that conception, that theme—those things are what brought *Filter House* to the attention of the Tiptree Award Jury. In a letter you sent earlier this summer, you said that having read my interview at *Fantasy Magazine*, you finally understood that my stories were a gift to you. I hope this means you realize now the crucial part you play in my work. If you ever need that reinforced, just read my "Statement of Intent"—I've appended it to this letter to make sure you've got a copy.

Gina thought of having you attend WisCon with me. She knew it would be a treat for both of us, and that adding the rest of the household—her and her kids—would have been too much.

Road trip with June! I had to get in an argument with you to be allowed to spend the money the Tiptree Motherboard had allotted me for travel expenses. But that was just a little fight set in a big, broad swathe of wide-open roads, rolling prairies, and contented companionship. Then we were in Madison, and then we were in the lobby of the Concourse Hotel, and then we were in WisConLand. I got to introduce you to everyone there: "This is my mom!" I let them all know they were lucky to be meeting you.

Mom, I was so proud! Your first foray into fandom, but I knew you would take it by storm. A lifetime of code-switching paid off, and you seemed equally at ease with academics and artisans, luminaries and librarians, journalists and jewelers and award jurors, because you were. You carried your comfort with you, and you wore it the way people say I wore my tiara: naturally, as to the manner born.

My favorite parts of WisCon 33 involved you. The Motherboard put us up on one of the Concourse's luxury-type floors, with free finger foods and a bar where I was shocked and delighted to watch you fending off the advances of a man my age—oh, you didn't think I was going to miss mentioning him, did you? No, I will never let you forget that you're sweet honey to the flies, because I hope to have the same reputation when I am 72 myself. And I *loved* that you loved the Tiptree auction, with its boobshake challenge and its chocolate vulvas, though you admitted ruefully you would never be able to explain it to anyone back home in Kalamazoo.

And then came the Tiptree Award Ceremony. We sat at the same table, enjoying scrumptious desserts. Before I knew it I was up on stage, receiving mighty mounds of swag: a pie, a shirt, a pin, a duck, a plaque, a song, a check for $1000. I had to make a speech; I'd expected I'd have to all along, and knew it should be short from prior experience as part of the audience. I think I thanked everyone I needed to, making many references to my list of acknowledgements in the front of *Filter House*, which list I idiotically advised people to read even if they didn't buy the book. And then I asked you to stand. And you did.

I told the hundreds of people in that ballroom "If there is any sweetness in what I've done, here is the source." They clapped for me. They clapped for you. They clapped for us, for a mother and daughter sharing knowledge and sweetness and accomplishment and acclaim. For the infinite series of reflections that arise when two mirrors face one another, when two women see themselves in each other. For the way they could see in us their mothers, their daughters, their sisters, their wives, their darlings, united in mutual admiration and mutual respect. For the power of women loving each other and honoring that love.

You sat back down, and so did I, and life continued on. It keeps doing that.

Thank you for giving me this life, and that sweetness, and for being with me during one of life's sweetest moments so far.

Love,

Nisi

Statement of Intent

Mother, I want to make something so beautiful, it would break a mean man's heart.

You have already made this thing. You call it the world.

But Mother, I want to make a little world like the big world you have made. Because the big world is too big. It's so big, mean men don't see it for what it is, even though the world is all around them. It doesn't break their hearts, or if it does, somehow they get this idea into their heads that because the world has broken their little hearts, then they ought to be able to break the big world.

If I can make a beautiful little world, then I can shove it under their noses. I can put this little world on a doily, put the doily on a plate and say see? See? You *do* see, you *do*, don't you?

Perhaps they will try to eat my world. Perhaps the beauty will break their teeth instead of their hearts. How ridiculous that would be.

Well, my world must not be so large small minds can miss it; yet it must not be mistaken for something to be swallowed whole, with impunity. It must be just the right size for having adventures in. The boundaries should be visible, but not so close that one is constantly bumping into them by accident.

It must be dear and sweet, and costly to approach, and well worth that cost. And it must be known even by those who never approach this world as a place that they have missed to their everlasting and eternal regret. Even its absence must affect.

Those who shun my world from fear will grow stronger and braver because of this lack. At last they will be able to face my world, and enter freely. Those who ridicule it will doubt their own wit, and will be ready to reverse their harsh sarcasms at the slightest hint of another chance, a reprieve, a renewed invitation to my world.

But most will come most willingly, drawn home to a strange familiar landscape, to a secret no one has told them, yet one they know quite well.

And Mother, they will call my world for you.

Bird Day

Nisi Shawl

We sat in a circle on the side of the street. Some of us had lawn chairs, or folding chairs we'd brought out from our houses. Step-stools, even. We had a bunch of different kinds of seats we were sitting in.

This was the day to commune with birds. It was a beautiful, cool, early spring morning. The pavement smelled clean and damp.

I was wearing a warm, comfortable caftan, embroidered with silver and dark colors. There were a lot of interesting-looking birds flying around low and purposefully, looking for the person they had a message for. It wouldn't do any good to get someone else's message, or to worry too much whether or not one was ever coming. We relaxed and watched the birds, and talked with neighbors who stopped by our circle. There were a few empty chairs. Eventually, someone might sit in them.

Suddenly, a bird approached me. It was a sort of bird I'd never seen before, a large duck with a sheeny, blue back, the blue of a clear sky just before dawn. I'd never seen a bird like this before, but I knew it was mine. It hovered awkwardly in front of me and gripped my index fingers with its webbed feet, pulling me. My heart lifted and I stood up.

The duck flew backwards, its feet still wrapped around my fingers. I went with it. It let go and turned to fly forward, and I followed it out of the city.

I wasn't about to let it get away from me. This was definitely my bird.

I saw a Great Auk from the corner of my eye, huge, black-and-white, with a broad, brightly-colored bill. It flew down a side road, but I stayed focused on my bird.

The paved road had turned into well-graded brown dirt, dark and wet. I saw houses that people were building: open, pleasing structures. I lost sight of my bird, but went on in the direction it had taken, out of the city. I stayed focused on it, even when I couldn't see it anymore.

I heard the soft beating of its wings and knew it flew on before me.

A stream joined me, running alongside the road. Daffodils joined the stream. Together, we left the houses behind.

I kept walking. I couldn't see my bird anywhere. I closed my eyes. The stream murmured to itself. The only beating I heard was my heart.

How could I catch up? Without wings, how could I fly?

I opened my eyes again and looked around. Where was I? Maybe this was where my bird had been bringing me. Maybe it had left me where I was supposed to be.

Tall trees with their leaves just beginning arched over the road. It was really more a wide path than a road, now. It moved among the tall trees slowly, one way, then another, quite casually. As if it knew where it was going, but felt no rush to get there.

This didn't seem like a place to stop at, an end.

Maybe my bird had left me because I would be able to figure out everything on my own from here.

I saw sky through the trees. I went at the path's pace till I came to their edge.

It was quite an edge. Only clouds beyond. Very beautiful clouds, with popcorn-colored crests and sunken rifts full of shadows like grey milk.

It was evening already. I could tell by the light. I had been following my bird all day. How had that happened? I had lost track of the time.

That didn't matter, though.

My bird did matter. And its message for me.

It had to be around here somewhere.

The clouds' lighter parts changed and became the color of the insides of unripe peaches. Against them rose black flecks, the flocks of birds flying away from us. Away once more, until next year.

Silence stirred the hairs on the nape of my neck. Silence and a small wind fanned them so they extended upward. And outward. Up and out. Above my head, my bird flew forward, over the edge.

I went with it.

“26 Letters to WisCon”

My WisCon #3

Julie Andrews

A is for Art Show, full of really cool stuff. Dragons and kittens, beautifully-sized women, science, fantasy, and real world blending. Plus Baba Yaga’s house. How cool’s that? Don’t forget to buy a Tiptree shirt.

B is for Books. Books from small publishers, books from small bookstores, books by Broad Universe broads. Buy in the dealer’s room, or a Room of One’s Own. Buy from local used bookstores if you don’t have enough yet. But buy the GoH books well before Sign Out!

C is for Clarion classmates. And Clarion instructors. And Clarionites from other years. Share a room, share a panel, share a reading, but definitely share a meal.

D is for Dessert Salon. No one told me my first year that the tickets were cool. Two desserts worth the money. Fruit, chocolate, and cream. Next year, wait in line for a good seat near the speeches.

E is for Everyone. Fans of all genders, all sizes, all colors, all abilities. All friendly and brilliant and worth having a chat with.

F is for Fried Cheese Curds. Seriously? Fried? Fat, salt, and more fat, but still appealing. Somehow.

G is for Green Room. Not for the privileged few; just volunteer for a panel. Has some of the best food, but the fruit disappeared.

H is for Hotel. Not to be neglected. Free shuttle, free Internet, a lounge on each floor. The rooms are cold, but the staff are not.

I is for Input, given at all stages. Suggest a panel, suggest 10. Request to be a panelist on others. Offer to moderate one. Make it happen. When it’s all over, give feedback for next year.

J is for James Tiptree Jr. Award. Better yet, the Auction. Miss whatever panels, readings, and programming you must, but don’t miss the Auction. Someday, once richer, bid on cool stuff.

K is for Kids. Kids at the con, kids at the panels. One year, hopefully soon, kids on the panels.

L is for LiveJournal. Join the community, learn what's going on, find a ride or a roommate. Liveblog a panel, read and write con reports. Discussions. Drama! Next year, invade Twitter.

M is for Market, if you remember to go. Local produce and plants, plushies and shirts. Some year, maybe, I'll buy and not just look.

N is for Ninety-Minute Panel Blocks. Time to discuss, to have fun, to get interested and sustain interest, to ask questions, even if shy. Time then to escape, to relax, to breathe, to quick buy a book. To get to the next panel without being late. Well...not *too* late.

O is for Organizers, who do a ton of work. Help them out, volunteer, appreciate them, and give feedback.

P is for Pocket Program, the most awesome thing ever. See timelines, descriptions, panelists. Plan your whole con, or decide on the fly. Easy to carry, difficult to destroy. All hail the mighty pocket program!

Q is for ________. (See **I** above. What *does* **Q** stand for this year? Let me know.)

R is for Restaurants. A shame to go back to one more than once, but something different every trip. Food is excellent, interesting, exciting. Company is even better. Try the tapas, and the pizza, and the daal. Oh, and the hummus. Wait, did someone suggest burgers?

S is for Secret Feminist Cabal. Where ### and ### domination ### planning ###. Next year, be sure to ###.

T is for Transportation. Shuttle to hotel, must wait, very busy. Fellow WisCon attendees? Awesome. Hi. Is this your first WisCon? Hey, didn't I see you on the plane? WisCon has begun!

U is for Unicorns...nahh. **U** is for Unbelievably Awesome Panels. The best part of the con. Amusing titles, intriguing descriptions, incredible panelists, and thought-provoking thinky thoughts. Take many notes, but pay attention too. Meat volcanoes and Captain Jacks. Annoying tropes and bisexual vampires. Then reading lists, reading lists, reading lists.

V is for Veggie Dogs. In the Consuite, carbs and protein when most needed. Small and chewy? Still, free food! Hmmm...maybe **V** can stand for popcorn. That's even better. And remember to Volunteer. Consuite staff can always use the help.

W is for Women. They're everywhere. On concom, on panels. Asking questions, giving answers. Talking, being heard. Listening, sharing. One or two of them may even write science fiction.

XY is for Men. They're everywhere too. More than I expected. Moderating, chairing, volunteering. Active, engaged, listening. That doesn't mean I went to WisCon to meet a guy, Mom.

Z is for Zat's All. See you next year!

*Format inspired by Jane Yolen's "The Alphabetics of Story" and "The Alphabetics of Writing" in *Take Joy: A Writer's Guide to Loving the Craft* (Cincinnati, OH: Writer's Digest Books, 2006).

Julie Andrews is a writer, a reader, and an out and proud geek. Also a Clarion grad, a library assistant, a new Broad Universe member, an even newer Outer Alliance member, a perpetual student, and smug owner of the shortest short bio in the WisCon 33 pocket program.

Rethinking Disabling Metaphors

Panel report by Sandy Olson

> Insults and epithets are pervasively framed as physical and mental differences, such as "they are blind to needed change and deaf to reason." These unconscious metaphors strongly influence how people with actual disabilities are perceived—by the world and by ourselves. This highly–interactive session will include role play and brainstorming to identify these disabling metaphors, deconstruct their logical errors, and invent more accurate, yet still powerful alternatives.
>
> Panelists: Jesse the K (Moderator), Elise M, Sandy Olson, Georgie L. Schnobrich

This panel was really fun, with great panel and audience participation. We started with a "language amnesty" declared by our mod, meaning we were going to throw around words that might offend some of us, and talk about why they are offensive, and come up with new words that might replace them.

Sometimes in arguments or discussions, we might object to a statement by saying something like:

How lame!
That's crazy talk!
That's retarded!

Jesse asked us what words "burn our cookies the most." Elise doesn't like "stupid" because it is part of a general privileging of a certain type of intelligence, and being smart doesn't automatically mean one is right, or ethical, etc. She also doesn't like "lame" and suggested that it's so prevalent because it has become an accepted replacement for "gay" on the playground—a word you won't get punished for using.

Georgie doesn't like how "crazy" is an automatic dismissal, a way of making one's self feel comfortable again when one is uncomfortable.

The audience came up with many others: spaz, psycho, short bus, retarded, blind, deaf, dumb, idiot, moron, cretin (the last three are words that used to be medical terms for the developmentally disabled). Some discussion ensued about kids using words on playgrounds, and how we might stop these insults—by coming up with new metaphors, or by generally making society more accepting of disability? (I don't think it's an either/or—I think it's tied together, and we do both at once.)

There was also some discussion of the appropriate use of terms—when is it OK to say crazy or paranoid. Certainly running upstairs to get away from the axe-wielding man in the horror movie is not wise and perhaps even crazy behavior. Thinking every car on the road is out to get you is paranoid. But overusing these terms can be insensitive and also might take away from their real clinical meaning (as with depression). Also someone mentioned how people will say "OCD" as a way of joking about being clean, but that's insensitive to people who do have OCD and know that it's not a happy, fun thing to have.

Mary Anne Mohanraj was in the audience and made some great comments about how it can be sad to lose some of these terms, because they are rich terms with a lot of meaning—she used "gypped" as an example. But she doesn't really need another term for "cheat" (why not just say cheat?), and the political gain is worth it.

Then we came up with many new terms to replace the ones on our list. Silly, ridiculous, foolish. "Let's talk more like Jane Austen," Georgie said at one point, making the audience laugh. Elise suggested that when you have to insult someone, why not just call an asshole an asshole? She also said that if you need to insult someone, please watch out for the collateral damage: who else are you hurting with your words, besides your target?

Here are a few of the suggestions the audience came up with:

> You're just planting weeds!
> That's burnt stew! You can't even boil water!

Rancid, putrid, spoiled, uncooked
Some already exist:
doesn't have a row to hoe, can't hold water
Out of tune
Sand in the gears
buggy (as with computers)
blue screen of death
epic fail
the potato salad of your reasoning is rancid (an audience favorite)
ridiculous as a replacement for retarded (because it conveniently starts with the same letter).

Commenters on LiveJournal came up with other examples:

All hat and no cattle
Has kangaroos in the top paddock (an Australian term)

At the end we talked a bit about reclaiming negative terms. People within the group always have more freedom to use terms (like "gimp" and "crip") than those outside of it.

I talked about "crutch" as a metaphor. "You're using X as a crutch" is usually used as a negative, as a criticism, as if crutches are bad, and as if they are optional. First, crutches help people with disabilities get around. Second, people don't use them unless they need them! This metaphor gets at dependency as a bad thing (why aren't you standing on your own two feet), when in reality, crutches are just tools, like hammers. On the other hand, giving someone a lift, a leg up, or a boost, all are good metaphors! So I propose that we all start using the metaphor "good crutch." For example, Elise said, "I was really happy to have work as a crutch to help me through a grieving process." Later in the weekend, General Jinjur referred to her OTW (Organization for Transformative Works) buttons as a good crutch for assisting her in talking to people.

Also later in the weekend, Cat H. mentioned "brainstorm" as ableist language, because it a) refers to epilepsy and b) privileges thinking quickly. One alternative is "rapid idea generation" or "rigging."

Jesse and I had planned on talking about "somatic metaphors" and why they are not necessarily ableist, but we did not have time for this during the panel.

Some examples of somatic metaphors are:

Standing tall, standing up for yourself
Taking steps in the right direction
Seeing someone's point
Being on your toes

These metaphors are rooted in our common existence as creatures with bodies and do not necessarily contribute to a disabling society, although the difference between a neutral somatic metaphor and disabling language is slippery at best (to use another somatic metaphor).

Thanks to our wonderful audience members! We had great participation and were thrilled to see the discussions that ensued throughout the convention and on the internet.

Sandy Olson likes sf/f books and shows, fanfic, digital photography, science, horses, and coats. She's attended three WisCons so far and likes talking about Access. She lives in Madison.

Up Off Our Couches: Mental Illness Activism and Speculative Fiction

JoSelle Vanderhooft

> "I wouldn't want to read a story with a protagonist who has depression. How is a character who just sits on the couch all day interesting?"

An audience member made the above statement—more or less, remembering the exact wording is hard eighteen months later—during a 2008 WisCon panel on disability representation in speculative fiction, in response to my frustration over the dearth of mentally ill characters in science fiction and fantasy.

And I was stunned; too stunned to think of a good reply.

Over twenty years of living with clinical depression and an anxiety disorder—which often follows the first like a rabid terrier—and I had no good words to debunk this assertion. This woman's words cut through the panelists' table—that bastion of authority even at such a democratic convention—like a band saw. I clenched my fists and began sweating. I felt my heart speed up and the cold trickle down my arms—a feeling of panic with which I am all-too familiar. I felt shamed, dismissed, diminished. And I felt angry.

That anger has been percolating for eighteen months now. It has resulted in several LiveJournal posts exploring my life as a depressive,[1] systemic social fear and hatred towards those with

1 While I agree that using people-first language when it comes to people with mental illnesses (e.g., "person with schizophrenia" rather than "schizophrenic") is always the best thing to do, I identify as a depressive rather than a person with depression. I do so because explaining my life is impossible without mentioning that I have lived with active depression since the age of seven. To me, it is an aspect of identity, just as I am also queer, right-handed, brown-eyed, and of primarily Dutch, Armenian, and US American heritage.

mental illnesses (which I refer to as "psychophobia" rather than the older term "stigma" for reasons I will explain shortly), and the ways in which psychophobia manifests itself in activist discussions. And, of course, this essay, which I consider to be a combination of all three.

Basically, I'm just sick and tired of having to navigate an oppression that many people—including activists and even many individuals with mental illnesses—can't or don't want to see. I hope this essay can help you understand.

✷ A Caveat ✷

Before we begin, however, I think it is important to note that this essay will be limited in scope not just because mental illnesses affect people differently, but because mental illnesses are not all alike, even when their symptoms overlap. A sidewalk crack, for example, exists between clinical depression in the categories of "mild," "moderate," and "severe." Between clinical depression and its milder cousin dysthymia (which I often describe to people as the equivalent of walking around with a low-grade fever for months or years at a time) that crack is more like a rain gutter. Between clinical depression (unipolar depression) and bipolar disorder (formerly manic depression), that gutter becomes a highway. Between clinical depression and more severe illnesses like schizophrenia, that chasm might as well be several neighborhoods away.

While our concerns overlap—because our symptoms often do, and because psychophobic and ignorant society often makes no distinction between us—we nonetheless have different challenges, different needs, different oppressions. I would also hazard to say that privilege works differently among us. Clinical depression, for example, is the mental illness people are most likely to understand because of its prevalence and the press time it has received in the past twenty years. Bipolar disorder, on the other hand, is socially less understood and more feared. Schizophrenia, which is even more stereotyped and less understood, is more feared than both. I am more likely, then, to be understood as a depressive than as someone with bipolar disorder, by individuals, by health care providers, and by society at large.

Further, while the concerns about which I speak impact all people with mental illnesses, this essay will inevitably skew towards a depressive's—and an individual depressive's—take on things. Finally, the term "mental illness" is also a problematic one that I dislike because it implicitly denies the biological component of these illnesses.[2] However, to date I have not found another term that is both accurate and socially recognizable enough to use in its place. "Brain disorder" seems too broad, and "psychiatric diagnosis," while much more appealing, is incorrect—not only because many people with mental illnesses never visit a psychiatrist, but also because psychiatric diagnoses are often incomplete or incorrect. So, unfortunately, until a better term presents itself, I must stick with the least of several bad options.

What is Psychophobia?

As I have struggled to come into my own as an activist, my thinking about society's treatment of people with mental illnesses has changed drastically. At first, I used the terms (dis)ablism and stigma, although neither seemed adequate to me. I think an explication of the weaknesses of both is useful when it comes to discussing mental illness.

(Dis)ablism,[3] as I suspect most readers are aware, is the systemic, societal, and institutional privileging of able-bodied people over people with disabilities. Immediately, this word becomes problematic when applied to people with mental illnesses. Although the brain is very much a part of the body, people often do not consider the outpourings of the brain—intellect, emotion, memory, and all other trappings of consciousness—to have a biological component. Thus comes the old

2 The debate over whether mental illnesses are biologically based or environmentally triggered is a large one, and a debate that could comprise an essay of its own. For brevity's sake, then, I subscribe at least in part to a biological view of mental illness, and that view informs this essay.

3 Disablism appears to be the preferred term in the United Kingdom, while most United States readers seem to prefer ablism. For clarity's sake—and because I have no preference between either—I use a parenthetical.

canard about the split between mind and body. And while mental illnesses frequently impact the body beyond the brain through symptoms such as fatigue, insomnia, psychomotor retardation or agitation, and even facial tics, few people appear to make the connection. This often leads to people with mental illnesses being unwilling or unsure if they can truly be categorized as disabled. Despite, for example, depression being a leading cause of disability across all nations and cultures, according to the World Health Organization.[4]

This problem became abundantly clear to me earlier this year, during the annual "Blog Against Disablism Day." In a post dated April 13, 2009, the organizer of the event (held annually at the blog "Diary of a Goldfish" wrote:

> Every year I have been asked, so it's worth saying; the discrimination experienced by people with mental ill health is disablism, so naturally such posts are welcome too.[5]

The very fact that the blogger—known only as "The Goldfish"—had to write this sentence indicates, to me, that enough people do not conflate mental illness with disability as to make (dis)ablism a less than effective term. Further, given that many people with mental illnesses are invisibly disabled (that is, some of us can often "pass as normal") and that some even choose to shun such descriptors as "disabled" and "disability," I think (dis)ablism, while accurate, is far too broad for this very specific oppression.

While (dis)ablism is too far reaching, I think "stigma" does not reach far enough. The Mayo Clinic, a "not-for-profit medical practice" that frequently treats people with mental illnesses, provides one of the best definitions of stigma I have encountered:

> Based on stereotypes, stigma is a negative judgment based on a personal trait— in this case, having a mental health condition. It was once a common perception that having a mental illness was due to some kind of personal weakness. We now know that mental health disorders have a biologi-

4 http://www.who.int/mental_health/management/depression/definition/en/

5 http://blobolobolob.blogspot.com/2009/04/blogging-against-disablism-day-will-be.html

> cal basis and can be treated like any other health condition. Even so, we still have a long way to go to overcome the many misconceptions, fears and biases people have about mental health, and the stigma these attitudes create.
>
> Stigma may be obvious and direct, such as someone making a negative remark about your mental health condition or your treatment. Or it can be subtle, such as someone assuming you could be violent or dangerous because you have a mental health condition.[6]

The problem with this term is that it does not clearly emphasize the historical and societal bases of discrimination against people with mental illnesses. The key words, I think are "common perception," "misconceptions, fears [and] biases." These words, along with words like "prejudice" obfuscate the issue. They make it sound like discrimination, fear, and hatred towards people like me is an individual thing, that there isn't a centuries-long history of bad science, bedlams, and domination to back up this "common perception." I wonder, indeed, how this article's author thinks "common perceptions" come about if not through the building blocks and cement of history?

And, really? "Once a common perception that having a mental illness was due to some kind of personal weakness?" *Once*? I'm sure people whose so-called "loved ones" scold us for being lazy, worthless, and faking it when we're at our lowest are comforted to know that this perception is no longer "common." Try harder, guys.

While the term "psychophobia" has its limits (which are quite close to the objections many gay rights activists have raised over the term "homophobia"), it comes the closest for me in putting this mistreatment in its proper place: alongside other social oppressions like sexism, racism, heterosexism, ageism. For me, this term identifies the mistreatment and discrimination against people with or perceived to have a mental illness as much more an insidious force than a "common perception" held by the unenlightened. Psychophobia, like homophobia before it, implies not only an institutionally-approved form of discrimination and a power differential between those (apparently) without mental illnesses and those who have them. I find

6 http://www.mayoclinic.com/health/mental-health/MH00076

myself deeply frustrated that more mental health advocacy groups have not adopted this term. In fact, I find little evidence that they are even aware of its existence!

So, too, is the population at large unaware. Indeed, the first page of a Google search for "psychophobia" brings up a Black Sabbath song, an unrelated personal website, and a component of the videogame *Doom II*. Happily, it also turns up a blog post by one anti-(dis)ablism blogger who was instrumental in creating my awareness of the term.

Alison Hymes is the author of the Wordpress blog "Disability and Civil Rights Watch" (http://www.hymes.wordpress.com) on which she regularly posts about the discrimination and outright violence people with disabilities (including psychiatric disabilities) experience—particularly at the hands of hospitals and medical practitioners. As part of the 2008 Blog Against Disablism Day, Hymes, a retired outpatient therapist who has post-traumatic stress disorder, wrote "Psychophobia 101," the best primer on this oppression I have yet encountered.

While I recommend readers visit her blog to read the complete post, I excerpt the parts I found particularly relevant below:

> I define psychophobia as the fear and hatred of people with psychiatric diagnoses or those assumed or perceived by others as having psychiatric diagnoses....
>
> Psychophobia is most visible in the media and TV and movies, but it is just as present in everyday life. It is present when employers refuse to interview or hire someone who is otherwise qualified because of a psychiatric history.... Psychophobia is ubiquitous in political writing and discussions where the opposition, left or right, is so often called some version of insane. ...
>
> Psychophobia demoralizes people with psychiatric diagnoses. It may demoralize them before they even obtain a diagnosis because once they do, all those horrible things they heard their entire life about "those people" can come back to them and seem to apply to themselves now. Psychophobia encourages people with mental illness to isolate, to hate themselves, and to identify with folks who put them down

> and hurt them. Psychophobia has allowed doctors and nurses to use torturous "treatments" on people in psychiatric hospitals for more than a century and into the present day....
>
> Psychophobia kills, demoralizes, and oppresses all of us.[7]

This is the definition of psychophobia from which I will work for the duration of this essay.

Psychophobia and Speculative Fiction

Unfortunately, speculative fiction, film, and television have made several contributions to this feedback loop, in much the same way they have contributed to sexism, racism, and heterosexism (formerly homophobia). Think of all the horror movies that hinge upon whether or not the lunatic will kill the innocent teenagers summering in the remote cabin. The fantasy books where the villain who wants to take over the world has "crazy" as his only motivation. The scores of mad scientists screaming "It's alive! Alive!" Think of Renfield who grants Count Dracula access to Mina Harker and ultimately becomes his victim in *Dracula*. Think of the Joker and possibly even Two Face from the Batman franchise.

Although I tend to be quite ambivalent about the Joker—depending on the medium in which he appears and who is writing him—I could understand why Heath Ledger's portrayal in *The Dark Knight* offended many mental health advocates. After all, Ledger's Joker is ruthless, sadistic, violent, and entirely lacking in empathy towards his dozens of victims: traits often attributed to mentally ill characters.

In August 2009, the Time to Change Campaign, a UK-based program to end discrimination against people with mental illnesses, released a report criticizing Hollywood's portrayal of people with schizophrenia. The report's author, Newham University Hospital's Dr. Peter Byrne, particularly singled out *The Dark Knight*.

---

7 http://hymes.wordpress.com/2008/04/30/blogging-against-disablism-day-post-psychophobia-101/. I also recommend Hymes' 2009 BADD follow-up, "Psychophobia 201," which can be read at http://hymes.wordpress.com/2009/05/01/psychophobia-201/.

"Batman describes the Joker as a schizophrenic clown, and when the film's second hero Harvey Dent becomes 'Two-Face' and embraces evil, the familiar stereotype of schizophrenia is activated," he told the *Telegraph* on August18. "The incorrect stereotype in both cases, to a lesser and greater extent, is that schizophrenics have multiple personality disorder, and that that second personality is always evil.... This is omnipresent in cinema misrepresentations—the psycho killer is immortal [sic?] and sadistic, motivated by madness and in almost all psychosis films that character will kill."[8]

Although Byrne is dead-on about these psychophobic representations of people with schizophrenia,[9] either he or the reporter misidentified the person who called the Joker schizophrenic. It was not Batman, but rather Ledger himself in a 2007 *New York Times* interview. Here Ledger told journalist Sarah Lyall that his character was a "psychopathic, mass-murdering, schizophrenic clown with zero empathy."[10]

This is really just as bad. The late actor confused two separate diagnoses: antisocial personality disorder (formerly psychopathy) and schizophrenia. While not all sociopaths are mass-murderers (and not all mass-murderers are sociopaths), they are, indeed, unable to empathize with others—a fact which makes the majority of them difficult to treat and legitimately dangerous to others (though through no fault of their own). Contrary to psychophobic stereotypes,

8 http://www.telegraph.co.uk/health/healthnews/6043231/Heath-Ledgers-Joker-exacerbates-stereotypes-about-mental-health.html.

9 However, I would quibble with him about his interpretation of Harvey "Two-Face" Dent. While he has often been played or portrayed as mentally ill in other movies and comics, I did not think this was the case at all in *The Dark Knight*. However, I did take issue with the portrayal of Dent's being "driven insane" by his girlfriend Rachel Dawes' murder—and not only because of the "women in refrigerators" phenomenon. Although reactions to trauma (in this case, Dawes' murder and Dent's disfigurement) are as individual as the people going through trauma, trauma does not usually drive people—particularly upstanding people like Dent—to murder and mayhem. I call this phenomenon in many films and TV programs "psycho shorthand," and it is an example of psychophobia of a different kind: inaccuracy.

10 "http://www.nytimes.com/2007/11/04/movies/moviesspecial/04lyal.html?_r=1.

schizophrenics are not unable to empathize and are rarely dangerous to others. In fact, they are more likely to be victims of violence. In fact, the two disorders exist on two completely separate diagnostic axes,

Understandably, such fine distinctions can be confusing, particularly to laypeople, and I do not expect Ledger or anyone else to be an expert. I do, however, expect them to realize that people with schizophrenia and anti-social personality disorder are still people, and that lumping them together, and equating them basically with violence, does all of society a grave disservice. And while I would not necessarily classify Ledger's Joker as schizophrenic (sociopathic, certainly), I think it is safe to assume that Ledger's understanding of mental illness as violent, selfish, and harmful to others went into his character and came across to many who viewed *The Dark Knight*. Unintentionally or not, his Joker became part of the psychophobia that leads to the culture-wide misunderstanding of people with schizophrenia. And all too often that misunderstanding leads to their mistreatment and neglect, and even to their deaths.

Even the best-intentioned media often fails people with mental illnesses. And here, I criticize a TV show that I adore: *Avatar: The Last Airbender*. Now, *Avatar* is a remarkable program in the racist and sexist morass that is common US television. Although created by two white men, it features a cast of entirely Asian and Inuit-inspired characters and does not disrespect the cultures from which it draws—at least, as far as this white woman can tell. Its female characters are, for the most part, well-rounded, active, strong, and not objectified. Its analysis of such weighty topics as sexism and colonization is remarkable, particularly for a cartoon aimed primarily at the seven- to twelve-year-old demographic. Its storyline is engaging, tense, and deeply affecting.

And whenever I hear gentle, kind, and awesome Uncle Iroh say of his niece Azula, "She's crazy and she needs to go down," I honestly feel like throwing up.

Azula is the fifteen-year-old daughter of the *Avatar*'s imperialistic Fire Lord and one of the show's many remarkable women. In season two, her father sends her to track down the Avatar, the only person who can stop his drive to conquer the world. To trap her quarry and advance her beloved father's agenda, Azula resorts to deception, violence, attempted murder, and exiling her two close friends when they dare to oppose her plans. She is cunning, ruthless, a prodigious fighter, and, in many ways, a borderline sociopath—borderline because she genuinely loves her friends, her emotionally abusive father, and her long-vanished mother, who she believes always saw her as a monster.

After her friends betray her and her father becomes increasingly distant and obsessed with his war effort, Azula experiences a psychotic meltdown, complete with hallucinations, paranoia, and unprovoked bouts of rage. Her transformation from cool, possessed warrior to frightened, ill teenager is astounding to behold and quite believable clinically. Yet, at the same time, I winced as I watched Azula smash the mirror in which she hallucinated seeing her mother's face. From decades of absorbing psychophobic media, I knew things were not going to end well for her.

And of course, they did not.

In "Sozin's Comet," the four-part series finale, a completely overwhelmed Azula is about to be crowned Fire Lord after her father crowns himself "Phoenix King" over all the world. Her coronation is interrupted, however, by her older brother Zuko, and Katara, another of the series' heroes. A dramatic battle ensues, in which the two friends defeat Azula. As I watched her writhing on the ground, chained, crying, and thoroughly broken, I realized that the show had exceeded my worst fears. Once again, here was a character with a mental illness who was still, ultimately, a threat to be put down no matter how sympathetic and human the show's writers made her.

I find it telling, also, that Azula is the only character (aside from her father, of course), who doesn't end happily, or even at all. After the battle, we never see her again. Nickelodeon's *Avatar* website informs us that she has been sent to a "mental health facility." To that I can only say, *seriously*? The anachronism notwithstanding,[11] the term "asylum" is incredibly loaded. While things have changed

11 I find the existence of such a western, post-Victorian concept as mental hospital in Avatar's Qing Dynasty and feudal Japan-inspired world to be...well, sort of tacked on, to say the least. The Nickelodeon website also regrettably identifies Azula's behavior as "a little nutty"—a psychophobic insult. While the creators of the show likely did not write this description, it still should not have appeared in official media at all—specifically official media intended for children and teens, many of whom also have mental illnesses!

a lot from the seventeenth century bedlams, such facilities (including hospital psychiatric wards) are frequently places where patients suffer sexual abuse, forced treatments, and a number of other indignities. So while I believe the creators meant Azula's incarceration to be a helpful and hopeful thing, the implications to anyone who has ever been sent to one of these places (or lived with the fear that they could be) are chilling.

I bring up these examples not to shame or scold *The Dark Knight* or *Avatar*'s creative teams but rather to point out, well, examples. The problems of psychophobia in speculative media go far beyond any individual film, book, or show, and far beyond any individual's power to single-handedly change, just as psychophobia in society at large is impossible to change individually. Happily, though, improving our stories and our society go hand in hand.

Psychophobia and Other Activism

Not as happily, I have seen a lot of psychophobia in action in our community's other activist circles, particularly in online discussions about racism, sexism, and heterosexism. During 2009's extended RaceFail, to cite one example, I often saw people calling out racism referring to those who showed it as "crazy," "insane," "nuts" or any other permutation of these insults. Those called out for racist language, of course, responded in kind. After author John C. Wright wrote his (now deleted) LiveJournal screed against gays and "homosex" on July 29, some bloggers criticized him by calling him senile and mentally ill.

To fight psychophobia, the first thing we as activists can do is to stop using psychophobic insults. This may seem obvious, but given the pervasiveness of words like "lunatic" and "nuts" in our vocabulary, it's often easy to miss, especially if you have non-mentally ill privilege. As I explained on my own LiveJournal shortly after Wright's post:

First of all, [doing this] makes racism/sexism/homophobia/etc. something that "those people" do, and not actual social problems with deep, thick, ugly roots that anyone with privilege is responsible for perpetuating. This reasoning is ugly because it not only pathologizes these -isms, but because it further demonizes and "others" people with mental illnesses by saying that we're somehow more racist/sexist/anti-gay than "normal" people. I really shouldn't have to explain why this is total bullshit, but just in case I do: No mental illness has "being a bigoted, prideful, petty, and vicious asshole" as part of its diagnostic criteria. ... Having a mental illness doesn't make you less privileged or bigoted than people without mental illness, or less likely to own up to your privilege and bigotry.[12]

Next, ask yourself what you do and don't know about people with mental illnesses. Where does your knowledge come from? Have you read memoirs about dealing with depression or bipolar disorder? Watched a documentary about schizophrenia? Do you have any friends with mental illnesses (hint: you likely do)? Who have told you about their struggles? What are your thoughts and feelings about people with mental illnesses? Do you find them frightening, untrustworthy, incompetent? Do these ideas and feelings come from popular television or film? These may also seem like basic questions, but I have found them to be helpful, particularly in unpacking my own privileges. And as with unpacking any privilege, expect to do a lot of thinking and researching on your own; although many people with mental illnesses, like me, are willing to answer your questions and help you learn, we have busy lives that are made all the more complicated at times by our symptoms. Just like any other oppressed group, it is not our job to educate you, and we expect you to take responsibility for yourself, your privilege, and your mistakes. Do some more research, ask questions, and above all listen to people with mental illnesses when we tell you where you've made a mistake—and don't be defensive. After all, you are not a horrible person for growing up in a psychophobic society and absorbing its messages, but it is your job not to make that society even more psychophobic.

When you encounter characters who have (or who code as having) mental illnesses in SF/F/H, question those representations. Do they show people with mental illnesses as dangerous and violent, or as passive victims? What could SF/F/H be if people with depression, bipolar disorder, schizophrenia, and borderline personality disorder could be full parts of society? If you are a writer, what would this world look like if you envisioned it?

---

12 http://upstart-crow.livejournal.com/377812.html,

Up Off My Couch

I guess I could explain how I envision this world by finally answering that audience member's assertion of eighteen months ago. No, ma'am, characters with depression are very interesting. We are journalists and skateboarders, police officers and bakery owners, bus drivers and stage magicians, forest rangers and CEOs. We are black, brown, and white; male, female, both, and neither; straight, queer, and asexual; heroes and villains. We are your family, your friends, your co-workers, and your enemies. We are no more or less interesting or worthy of attention because we live with an illness, but we do not deserve your dismissal.

And also? No matter what TV and those annoying anti-depressant commercials tell you, we definitely do not sit around on our couches all day, every day, world without end, amen. I mean, I know it's hard to think through all the psychophobic feedback sometimes, but for God's sake! WAKE UP!

JoSelle Vanderhooft has published several collections of poetry, including *Fathers, Daughters, Ghosts & Monsters*, *The Memory Palace*, and *Ossuary*, a finalist for the 2008 Bram Stoker Award. She has also written one novella, *The Tale of the Miller's Daughter*. She lives in Salt Lake City, where she works as assistant editor of a gay and lesbian newspaper and spends any spare time collecting perfume, making jewelry, and playing with her cats.

Green Gables

Inspired by "The Unspunky Teen Protagonist"
WisCon, 2009, #71

Anne Sheldon

Being "spunky" never was a choice I made.
The line between me and obnoxious
was always thin.
Now a harried adult myself,
I shake my head when
older women smile,
remembering the "sprite"
who dyed her red hair green
and made Diana drunk
and broke a slate
upon the head of Gilbert Blythe,
but at the time there was no
talk of "plucky charm."
I think it fair to say
there was despair expressed
about my prospects.
This hurt — though
I can laugh about it now
with Gilbert
after a glass or two
of currant wine.

Bachelorae Antiquae

A meditation on "The Female Bachelor,"
WisCon 2009 #40

Anne Sheldon

They recline on sturdy Adirondacks
planted in a bright green lawn,
their pastel linen shirtwaists
freshly ironed—smart
happy old women surrounded
by adoring nieces and nephews.
Drinks in hand (Jane, dry sherry,
Nancy, a rum Coke),
they reminisce—the intricate cases,
mortal dangers, the breathless moments,
clever triumphs.

Now, of course,
there's arthritis,
more than one knee replaced,
and the roadster long ago traded in—
though Nancy still packs heat,
and Jane has defended herself
on more than one occasion
with a surprisingly sharp #9 needle.
They know they've missed forever
a few experiences
that might have expanded
wisdom—connubial sex, childbirth, etc.—

but you have to give up *something.*
They have no regrets.

Literature is a curious deception—
fans don't realize
they are about the same age,
considered themselves rivals, in fact,
but now they retire together
hand in hand.

Anne Sheldon's poetry has appeared in *Weird Tales*, *Spitball*, *Talebones*, and *Lady Churchill's Rosebud Wristlet*, as well as many mainstream journals; her fiction, in *Black Gate* and *Paradox*. Aqueduct published *The Adventures of the Faithful Companion*, a long poem based on Sumerian mythology, in 2005.

Haiku Earring Party

Elise Matthesen

> One by one, the stars
> Slide out through the wickerwork,
> Sparks limning her path.
>
> "A Basket Full of Sky" —Margaret Ronald

If I walked up to people at WisCon and said, "Write me a poem," many would look uncomfortable and tell me they didn't write poetry. I probably wouldn't get 12 to 20 percent of the convention membership writing. What I've learned from hosting the Haiku Earring Party is this: people will do all sorts of things, even commit art they might not usually dare, if they think they're getting free earrings out of it.

It starts like this: you wander down the sixth floor hallway, looking into party rooms. You find one with a long table holding pens and blank squares of cardstock. People sit there, writing intently or staring off into space thinking. Another table holds two hundred pairs of earrings, a dozen pairs, or something in between, depending on the hour. At the end of this table sits a woman with an unruly shock of short dandelion hair, holding a pair of pliers and a half-finished earring in her hands.

You study the table of earrings, looking for the pair that wants you. When they find you, you join the line that snakes toward the head of the table to show the woman with the dandelion hair your earrings.

By a quick process of divination, she gives you a title. (If pressed, she'll say yes, titles are made up on the spot, and yes, they have something to do with the earrings and something to do with the person, and also something to do with the words floating all around at that particular WisCon, the seedpod fluff that drifts off panels and conversations and discussions all day.) You take the earrings, sit at the table with the pens, and get to work.

Signs around the room explain the process, telling a bit about haiku and senryu. One says, "If you have formal poetry experience, it will not be held against you." You finish your poem and rejoin the line.

You reach the woman and hand your poem card to her. She reads it carefully, nods. "Put it where the earrings were. Then they belong to you. Oh, and please to put your name and email contact info on the back, yah? In case we need to contact you about permission to reprint." She grins.

After you put the card where your earrings started out, you stay to read a few of the other poems. The rest of the evening, between checking out noisy happy crowded other parties, you take little breaks in the room of earrings and poetry, looking for new poems that have bloomed on the table since you added yours. It's a dipper of cool water, a cupped double handful of creativity and calm. Sometimes mirth ripples around the earring table over a particularly amusing poem-card. Sometimes murmurs of conversation rise, cascade, and run down to murmurs again, but mostly the room is full of little noises of people writing and thinking, punctuated by the voice of the woman giving titles to people reaching the head of the line.

That woman is me, and the Haiku Earring Party is my favorite fun at WisCon. I love seeing people come in and take a chance. Things happen at Haiku Earring Parties, unexpected things, mixed in with the usual comfort and fun. One title brought a woman (a recent widow, I found out afterwards) to sudden tears and a precipitous exit without her earrings—and then back an hour later with a beautiful poem about her late husband. She was startled that I had held the earrings for her, but I would have held them for as many years as it took her to write that poem—I knew she was coming back.

I love being surprised by the poems. Most of all, I love the feeling of the roomful of people working. I love what they do, but even more, I love that they do it.

Each does it differently. Some use the earrings' title as first line. Vicki Rosenzweig did at the very first Haiku Earring Party in 2001:

So she told the duke
How the road runs south, and up,
As the clouds stream by.

Some use it as a poem title, like Janet Lafler did:

"The Secret Life of Bugs"
Pollen on my legs
In the heart of each flower
I leave a secret

The poems span genres and come in all flavors. Science fiction happens, like Jennifer Pelland's "The Sky Between":

Activate portal.
Look up, count stars, not enough.
Step through, try again.

Cherie Priest's "The Queen Kicks Some Ass" is modern fantasy:

Picky princess eats
Nothing from a tree, so I'll
Put it in a pie.

Nita Kelly brought one mythology home with "Persephone's Bar & Grill"—which could have been any small-town bar I knew growing up in Wisconsin:

Watch the game unfold
Eating hell-scorched ribs and steak
Six months of the year

Ellen Klages offers scientific ghost stories in "Antique Radio Waves":

Marconi is dead.
Emanations last longer
Than your frequency.

If you like your horror with humor, how about "Rockabye Monster" from Chris Waterous?

Wee fuzzy monster
Eyes wide, will not sleep.
Humans under bed!

Beth Meacham pointed out "The Trouble with Art Nouveau Spellbooks":

I have leaf, eye, toe
The cauldron is too lovely
To kindle a fire

And wherever authors, editors, publishers, agents, and the like have been discussing the stages of getting a book into print, there will be metacommentary like Greg Rihn's:

The ritual song
Of the copyediting tribe
Is a mournful one

I mentioned signs explaining how the Haiku Earring Party works. Over the years, I've added a little more information about what we're doing. Strictly speaking, most poetry at the party is not haiku; it's closer to something called senryu. For one thing, a true haiku needs a word that sets the poem in a particular season. I simplify wildly here; there are other guidelines, and also the vigorous debate that attends most living traditions. (I strongly recommend googling "modern haiku" and "traditional haiku," and finding out more about the deep rich history of haiku, senryu, and other Japanese poetic arts.)

Given the ongoing vigorous discussions on cultural appropriation, some of us wonder whether having a haiku earring party at WisCon—in which the so-called haiku are mostly senryu!—is cultural appropriation.

Those of us not at home in Japanese poetic culture would be foolish if we thought our unlearned, hazy-simplified-guidelines poems matched the formal intricacy and power of traditional Japanese haiku. But are we likely to do the tradition harm? This is a good question. I've gotten the strong impression that the notion we could do it harm would be, well, kind of hilarious to most Japanese people. How can I say it?

So polite: Iron
Chef, hiding a smile at my
Easy-Bake Oven.

Something like that, anyway. And that's an example of senryu. Senryu are poems with the syllabic structure and line patterns of haiku, but less formal and often humorous. See Beth Friedman's "Aliens at the State Fair," a personal favorite of mine:

Ride the donut machine
Eat fleece, flowers, and crop art
What do I try next?

Even if accidentally and ignorantly, we often wander toward the traditional guidelines. A significant number of the poems are anchored in a season, like Beth's State Fair poem or Greg Press's "Carnival of Flowers":

No acts here at noon
The roses wilt and pack up
The faire will leave soon

Senryu, haiku, or whatever, some have the excellent kick of Zen that delights me in certain celebrated Japanese haiku I have read in translation. Pat Murphy explains "How to Hide a Universe":

A difficult task,
Or so it might seem at first.
Then you close your eyes.

Or you can get there by going the other direction, says Amanda Lucek in "How to Discover the World":

To see it entire
First you must leave it behind
Make the stars your home

Some poems are crafted slowly over the course of an evening. Some are composed in the amount of time it takes to draw a breath, a task about as easy as drawing a perfect circle freehand. I gave Sharyn November the title "plant early for best results" and watched her walk to the window, turn, and come back to say:

of course, I mean seeds.
if you planted these earrings
nothing would happen.

Other poems get meta, like Cliff Winnig's "The Improved Wisdom of the Ancients":

Lengthy parchment scrolls
With epic sagas are out
We want a haiku

Little cards are easier to store than scrolls. I do keep all the haiku. They live in bags and envelopes in the big basket with other jewelry-related writing, in there with years of Artists' Challenge pieces, rubbing shoulders with poems like "William Morris, Genie (His Bottle)," a chapbook of ghazals from John Calvin Rezmerski, stories from many people, published and not, and a small rubber duck with purple tiara, which somebody gave me not too long after I donated a certain tiara to a certain literary award. Sometimes between WisCons I take out the haiku and run my fingers through them, reading randomly.

Poems in kanji, poems about spectral botanists, Francophile theorists.

Poems about long distance telepathy, Victorian mosh pits, the courage of leaves. Poems about history old, like "Cleopatra's Attitude" from Delia Sherman:

> Salad days behind,
> Octavian before me.
> Bring on the asps.

Poems about history recent, like Harry LeBlanc's "Yat* Faeries":

> Can't drown no fey, cher,
> But what you did to our town
> Army Corps must pay.

I read them on days I need to be reminded that there is art and fun in the world. When I need a little elixir of WisCon, I sift through the bags from Haiku Earring Parties past.

Mixed in with the earring poems are personal messages ("the panel was hard / and non-representational / you almost saved it"), notes about extra pliers, a haiku explaining why the writer isn't writing an earring haiku. One says "Late Saturday night / I lost at the auction. Damn. / I'm up here for snacks." A little sign in Mike Ford's calligraphic handwriting says "more earrings coming soon," from the year I forgot the earrings at home and we did new ones on the fly; intrepid helpers, equipped with pliers and fortitude and whatever beads we could find, saved the day. The stored assortment is better than any scrapbook, richer far than any one person could have composed.

Poems about Viet Nam, the Schwarzschild radius, obstreperous pixies, about what the bees know about history. Poems about mountains the poet grew up with and has not seen most of a lifetime. Poems about hope and dreams and loss and love and technology and magic, and where we are in the middle of all of them and where they are in the middle of all of us. Some fill my thoughts months later, like Vito Excalibur's "The Fossil Pecking Order":

The earliest are
Lowest. The desert swims with
Ghosts from ghostly seas.

Some make me giggle, like John Gamble's "Here Be Dragons":

Sulphur-crusted bones
Are scattered by the green van.
Childe Orkin parks hence.

A former honors mathematics major, I am especially delighted when someone writes mathematically literate poetry like Jessie Stickgold-Sarah's "The sweet longings of geometry":

Intercept my heart
By slow degrees, we prove love
From what is given

One thing isn't surprising, this being WisCon: a high percentage of feminist content, as "Cinderella's Pre-Nuptial Agreement" by Ariel Franklin shows:

This is how it goes:
No suds, no soot, no siblings,
And no silly shoes.

As I write this, I am about to turn forty-nine in a few short hours, and thus particularly appreciate Becca Schaffner's "Magic in the Fifties":

The joy of the crowd
Pales beside the sweet sharp glow
Of dancing alone

And with a fierce, fierce love, I love Evelyn Browne's "My Aunt the Tiger":

Her house has two doors.
When she's angry, she comes out
Through the other one.

As I said, I love the feeling of a roomful of people working. I'll do a lot to be in a room like that—like make a few hundred earrings and trade them for poetry. The Haiku Earring Party is a cousin to my

Artists' Challenges. Elizabeth Bear's Hugo winning short story "Tideline" was an Artists' Challenge from a necklace called "Sinner in the Hands of a Mildly Startled Buddha." A piece posted on LiveJournal called "Nine Things About Oracles" sparked more than a hundred different artworks. Inciting this stuff has been big fun for more than ten years now. Apparently other people enjoy it too: there's nothing like getting the news while recuperating from major surgery that one has been nominated for a World Fantasy Award "for setting out to inspire and for serving as inspiration for works of poetry, fantasy, and sf over the last decade through her jewelry-making and her artists' challenges." The Haiku Earring Party's a big part of that whole encouraging-other-people thing, and I'm grateful to WisCon for letting me do it.

Most years there are titles that elicit the comment, "How did you know to give that exact title to me? How could you know that?" The answer is that I don't know. I don't have to know. The titles find me, like the earrings find their people. All I have to do is pass them on. It's collaborative work, co-creation, playing telephone with art. It's one of the best games in the world, and I look forward to as many more Haiku Earring Parties at WisCons to come as I can manage. So wander down the sixth floor hallway through the open parties until you find a room full of quiet art-making. Just look for the table full of earrings and poetry, and the woman with the dandelion hair.

*A Yat is a nickname for a person from New Orleans who shares a particular traditional dialect. Guess where Harry's from?

Elise Matthesen lives in Minnesota, surrounded by beads, metal, words, music, and people she loves. She has a jewelry business, a hearing impairment, fibromyalgia, arthritis, attitude, ingenuity, numerous publication credits, and many pairs of pliers.

The "Doctor Horrible's Sing-Along Blog*" Party from WisCon 33

Britt Flokstra

Last year (WisCon 32, 2008) was my very first WisCon ever. I'm not sure how I missed the existence of this wonderful convention for such a long period of my life but, regrets aside, I am beginning to make up for missing the last ten years by throwing myself into the WisCon experience full force. At WisCon 33 (2009) I joined three panels and hosted a party. I expect to be back next year with even more participation.

Getting my bearings, learning the community style and setting my first year was fun; coming back this year and being able to more fully participate on panels and in programming was even better. So, if I write nothing else of importance in this article, please take home this: you don't have to wait a long time to become an active part of the whole WisCon experience.

I have been asked to write a bit about the Friday night "Dr. Horrible's Sing-Along Blog*" party I hosted at WisCon 33. My fifteen-year-old son actually came up with the idea of showing the musical to anyone at WisCon who might be interested. I thought that would be fun, so I ended up hosting a party showing the Joss Whedon Musical Masterpiece seven or eight times back-to-back. Including one brief showing of the extras!

Short background: when the writer's strike of 2007-2008 was in full force, Joss Whedon (amazing writer/producer of *Buffy the Vampire Slayer, Angel, Firefly, Serenity*, and *Dollhouse*) decided to make three fifteen-minute musical webisodes that told the story of a man who wanted to become a villain in the Evil League of Evil. Fans watched these three webisodes unfold over the summer of 2008. The following January, the full forty-five minutes was released to

DVD with extras. It instantly shot to the top of Amazon's DVD sales. This is the musical I showed all night long.

First, we decorated the party suite with scenes from the musical. I set up Dr. Horrible's lab in the area that had shelves and a sink. Since I teach chemistry, I had access to beakers, test tubes, flasks, and other exciting lab paraphernalia. I added food coloring to water and dry ice to the colored water for a bubbling, fun, evil laboratory set-up. Lots of people commented on how cool it was (cool for nerds—nerdtastic).

My son drew the laundromat, where Penny and Dr. Horrible (Billy) meet weekly to do their laundry, and hung it on one wall. Then we both designed the Evil League of Evil's (ELE) headquarters for the snack food and viewing areas. We had pictures of all the villains who are members of the ELE and announcements, sign-up sheets, and job openings for henchmen. We even made an application form for entry into the ELE that you could take with you.

Once the party started, we had between twenty and sixty people for each viewing until the wee hours of the morning. I cannot tell you how great it is to stand in a room with sixty people singing along and laughing with this incredibly well-made musical. Most parties at WisCon have people moving in and out and talking and sitting together, but in this party we bonded over the shared experience of singing and laughing (and perhaps even crying) together.

I had many people tell me that they had meant to get around to watching this, but hadn't made the time and were really glad I had brought it. I also had some Whedon fans that didn't even know about the musical and who planted themselves on the front row for several back-to-back viewings. I made new friends and had lovely conversations with fellow fans.

Throwing this party was a great way for me to introduce myself to the WisCon community. I had a wonderful opportunity to meet people who also love to sing and dance along to science fiction musicals. My son had a great time, too. He was dressed up as Dr. Horrible, and he made many new friends that night. I was tired for panels the next morning, but it was worth every moment!

I loved the ebb and flow of the WisCon participants as they came in at random places in the story and stayed on to watch it from the start, or those who watched and left and returned to watch again. It was a unique rhythm that marks a lot of what WisCon is like for me. The ebb and flow between panels, between parties, between meals, between friends, between conversations, like WisCon is a living, breathing, blood-pulsing entity. This party felt like part of the internal beat of that entity. We did not stand alone, but mingled together with the rest of the parties, panels, happenings, and life of WisCon.

Thanks, WisCon, for being such a great place for so many great people to meet and share experiences. I'll be back next year for more panels, parties, and that special essence that can only be found at WisCon.

*Dr. Horrible's Sing-Along Blog is written, directed, and produced by Joss Whedon. For more information please visit the official website http://drhorrible.com/.

Brittany Flokstra is a long-time sci-fi reader/watcher. *Star Trek, Babylon 5, Battlestar Galactica* and anything Whedon continue to keep her firmly on the sci-fi path. She has two BS degrees in Chemistry and Geology and her doctorate is in Environmental Science from the University of Iowa. She currently teaches chemistry at UNI while looking for a tenure-track position in her field.

WisCon and the Common Discourse

Meg Turville-Heitz

A retired couple sits on a worn couch in the Governor's Club lounge on a typical Saturday morning. A din of cups on saucers and the conversation of WisCon 33 members grabbing breakfast, consuming copious amounts of coffee and tea, and planning their schedule for the day, generate a background white noise to those who know WisCon. But for the retired couple, this is not typical background noise: snippets of party re-hash, of readings to be heard, of books read or ridiculed, of recollections about favorite authors and those maligned, of issues not resolved on the previous day's panels, of speculation on political or news events, of creative interpretations of all manner of the fantastic, and the moral implications of tropes. The coming and going attendees perch on chair arms, picnic on the carpeting and set up camp in front of the toaster. The couple's bemused smiles give way to questions. What is WisCon? Who are these people? How do you define speculative fiction and what does feminism have to do with it? Their eyes widen. Their smiles broaden. An eleven-year-old, my son Morgan, defines the genre for them with matter-of-fact precision and the addenda of a few nearby listeners. He discusses with them books they have read, and should read, and themes in them they might find pertinent to the con and feminism. The discussion grows animated, excited, as the participants connect ideas and form patterns they haven't seen before. Like so much of the discourse at WisCon, soon there are others gathering around and contributing, agreeing, disagreeing, coalescing, laughing, becoming that nebulous feeling of energy that is WisCon.

By the end of breakfast, the couple has met authors, editors, and fans, discovered they are among the latter and are already planning how they can attend next year, or at a minimum inform a son-in-law they are certain should be here.

It isn't the first accidental "discovery" of WisCon that has led to it becoming a ritual, like a holiday that has become a fixture on one's calendar that will be honored no matter what, with the planning often beginning at the end of the previous year's event.

During her guest of honor speech at WisCon 33, Ellen Klages noted how her first WisCon left her feeling as if she had finally found her tribe, a sense of belonging that brings her back year after year. It was about people who understood and asked similar questions and engaged in a level of discussion that just didn't seem to happen anywhere else. That sentiment has been expressed by many long-time WisCon attendees, Klages' reference to finding a tribe greeted by sage nods and smiles.

But just what generates that "tribe" feeling? If it's only once a year, can it be a tribal thing? The concept of a tribe suggests culture, a group with shared and socially transmitted patterns of communication and thought. Can an event that draws such a diversity of individuals with broadly different reasons for attending—from social to professional, producer to consumer—really be seen in such a unitary way that so many from such different social perspectives could see themselves as belonging? How does a shared interest become elevated to a ritual and annual re-bonding with a nebulous group that in many ways has nothing at all in common?

My son Morgan is one of those talking about the next WisCon before the present event has been put to bed. He talks about friends he sees only once a year who are critical to his social life. Somehow between the video games and constant consuite grazing, there is a social discourse, even among children, that rises above the ordinary.

"They're kind of like me," he explains. "They like the same kinds of things. They read the kinds of things I like to read. They actually know *how* to read. Most of my other friends don't even read."

It comes down to the people who have read in his genre and can talk about the books in a way that has yet to happen anywhere else in his experience.

I tried to get at that sense of what creates the ritual of WisCon attendance by asking a few people who only just recently made that surprising discovery of an event unlike any other and have added WisCon to their annual plan. I focused on a handful of people I met through Society of Children's Book Writers and Illustrator's membership, all of whom had only just recently begun attending WisCon. They were not coming to WisCon for the first time out of fandom, or necessarily from a long affiliation with the genre, or even because their many friends in the genre were all attending. Attendance was initially a professional, business, networking venture that delivered much more. In our discussions, it became clear that WisCon appealed not simply because through shared difference there is a sense of belonging—a common theme in many discussions at WisCon—but because it is also a place of open, multifaceted discourse where the secret handshake for entre to the tribe is a smile and the barriers are lowered between the professional and social.

For writer Georgia Beaverson, like several of her SCBWI colleagues, the first trip to WisCon (in 2006) was difficult because it meant overcoming shyness among a group in which she knew no one and finding an event that didn't match previous professional experiences. She had heard about the con from a variety of sources and thought she should be connecting with the genre as a writer of middle-grade fantasy. A reasonably priced convention in her home city was thus something of a given. But what began as strictly a professional interest now includes a social element.

"I like how committed people are to fantasy and science fiction," she says. "I can have a conversation (at WisCon) that I wouldn't necessarily have with the average friend and learn a lot about what I do." She notes that while the SCBWI members she knows well are professional, "there's a fierceness in the commitment of people who go to WisCon, to the writing and reading of [sf], that I don't see elsewhere." A sense of knowing everyone else's work and finding support among these other professionals has been a key feature of WisCon's appeal. She finds camaraderie among editors, agents, and authors that isn't necessarily evident in some other venues, as well as a real acceptance of everyone. She noted that the ability to be involved through panels and readings was less limited than at many more hierarchical events she's attended as a writer. The unique character of WisCon has positioned it among Beaverson's favorite professional conferences, and she has become a regular attendee.

Milwaukee-area writer Deborah Lynn Jacobs echoed Beaverson's sentiments about camaraderie and the sense of a supportive environment among professionals. Jacobs, who writes young adult fiction, discovered WisCon two years ago (2007) by word of mouth on the SCBWI-Wisconsin listserve. She was intrigued because of her own interest in science fiction, the feminist themes, and the idea that it could put her in touch with people who read what she reads and love what she does. At first worried that with attendance of 1000, the convention would feel too big, she said it ended up feeling small and cozy, filled with people who were interesting, knowledgeable, and easy to talk to, and with high quality programming that gave her the opportunity to learn a lot.

She notes that professionally WisCon has given her an opportunity to do a reading and be on panels despite being relatively unknown, something that emerges from a more democratic approach to programming. While it remains important professionally, she notes there's an appealing social element that emerges in the intensity of fans and "the camaraderie of people who have known each other for years and years. As if you are there with 1000 of your very best friends," and the kindness generated by that feeling.

Ingrid Kallick attended her third WisCon in 2009 to feed her professional interest as both an artist and writer. Kallick has found WisCon a way to connect with SCBWI members who have similar interests, as well as a way to move beyond some of the more formal professional discussions of other professional conventions to get into the cultural implications of the writer's work. She notes that the unique aspect of WisCon for her includes the conversation between the reader and writer. As an artist she was able to connect with people who were interested in her work, and has found WisCon an important way for her to connect writers and artists with publishers and consumers. Since it was an affordable event and in her home area, Kallick made the decision to go the first time solely as a professional outlet, but it has been evolving a more social function as she has come to know more people.

WisCon 33 marked the first attendance for Jacqueline Houtman, another Madison-area SCBWI member and writer, who says that she will definitely return. Like Beaverson and Kallick, she notes that the convenience and affordability of WisCon made it something of a no-brainer to attend, but now WisCon will be on her schedule and would be even if it wasn't so easy. Though she doesn't write speculative fiction and doesn't think of herself as an sf fan, she found something professionally meaningful about craft and marketing in every panel she attended. She figures the extensive program, open to everyone, has something for everybody. She couldn't image one typical type of attendee and found that the different interpretations and points of view that emerged throughout the convention made it unexpectedly socially and professionally useful.

For these attendees, as for me at my first WisCon sixteen years ago, the initial motivation was a professional connection outside of the general scope of the con. The unexpected outcome was the higher level of discourse and the social interactions with readers, writers, artists, and publishers who all communicate about cultural implications and social contracts, who speculate about the way things have been and what they might or should be.

Academic literature abounds with theoretical arguments for why we make rituals and seek the kinds of community WisCon represents. Ritual is argued to be a mnemonic device by which people remember their culture and connections, and reinforce that communal recall. Ritual can stand in for a form of communication or provide the setting for it. Here we come back to the themes that seem to emerge in so many testimonials of WisCon: the feeling of tribal connection. If we see tribe as a community with a shared culture and rituals with inferred social interactions and the transmission of ideas, then, in essence, it is the sharing of a common discourse—communicating using a shared repertoire of meanings in an exchange of ideas—that also creates community. Community emerges from the discourse, and the discourse is an integral feature of the ritual. This ritual that is WisCon annually celebrates, revisits, and reinforces the community.

Perhaps what defines the WisCon "tribe" is as broad as the ability to elevate the conversation to imagine and even embrace new perspectives.

Meg Turville-Heitz is pursuing her PhD in anthropology at the University of Wisconsin-Madison, and in her copious free time still writes and edits fiction and non-fiction, tries to operate a sustainable farm and raise an incorrigible son (the last most successfully).

Romance of the Robot: From *RUR* & *Metropolis* to *WALL-E*

Andrea Hairston

> *...the boundary between science fiction and social reality is an optical illusion.*
> —Donna Haraway

We're wiping our asses with the rain forest.

Or maybe it's the northern old growth forests that we're flushing down the toilet.

The World is indeed getting flat. Imperialism and colonialism have exhausted foreign, alien ground. The European invasions have succeeded. Everywhere on this planet is now *home* to Western Civilization (or too jacked up to be anything else)! So the imperial colonialists have jettisoned nationhood for virtual geography. We're all hapless natives of a bygone national era, regrettably getting stomped senseless by the inevitable march of progress. The relentless exploitation of worker-consumers and our precious material and spiritual resources is justified and glorified with religious fervor. As we are drowning, suffocating, poisoning ourselves in waste and greed, late model capitalism is worshipped as a religion, as the one true solution to the primal problem of distributing wealth. The magical, invisible hand of the market is considered godly in its ability to guarantee our dreams, our way of life, our continuation as a consumer species! Socialism, conflated with totalitarianism, is demonized, and any search for alternative economic systems is heretical, treasonous, and doomed.

Plain speech addressing these conditions is frequently ridiculed. Overt political art challenging the status quo is suspect—an artist can commit no greater sin than hitting us over the head with MESSAGES and spoiling our entertainment jones. Meanwhile, advertising sermons blare at us 24/7 from every possible surface, bandwidth, point of contact carrying a simple gospel message—you too can buy your way to happiness heaven!

This devastating present, glaring at us on the way to the multiplex, is the tragic past of *WALL-E*'s robot adventure/romance revolution. *WALL-E* is an almost silent film (especially in the beginning) and the eponymous robot character is a Chaplin clown figure, ironically compressing our tossed garbage into cubes and stacking them into skyscrapers. In the flat world of global capitalism, WALL-E is the cheapest of labor—powered by plentiful renewable energy—sunshine. For seven hundred years, this tramp-robot has built trash mountains, displaying not a moment of worker discontent with Buy N Large—the corporate dynasty last in charge. Robots are designed to be perfect workers. WALL-E seems no exception to that rule. Trundling through a desolate landscape, WALL-E sheds no tears for paradise lost, yet gathers unexpected treasures—including a sprout in a battered boot—and somehow survives when all other Waste Allocation Load Lifter Earth-Class robots have given up the ghost. Our plucky hero raids dead WALL-E models for spare parts and feeds a pet roach centuries-old Twinkies. The roach might be a robot too, but whether biological, mechanical, or cyborg, the bug is lovable, loyal, and as indestructible as the Twinkies.

At home under Christmas lights with pet roach feasting on pink icing, WALL-E watches a video of *Hello Dolly* and is enchanted by singing and dancing lovers before stacking himself on a revolving shelf to wait for morning. I say "himself," but WALL-E's gender is very much in the eye of the beholder. Roger Ebert in his review pauses analysis to mark the gender terrain, declaring, "He—the story leaves no doubt about gender—" while Kate Bornstein in her *Blog for Teens, Freaks and Other Outlaws* says,

> I'm completely smitten with WALL•E, this summer's Pixar/Disney offering. But the last thing I expected to see in my friendly, heterosexual upper east side Manhattan neighborhood movie theater was a feature length cartoon about a pair of lesbian robots who fall madly in love with each

> other. WALL•E is nothing short of hot, dyke Sci Fi action romance, some seven hundred years in the future! Woo-hoo!
>
> Isn't that what you saw?
>
> No? What movie were you watching?

Bornstein goes on to admit that at first she had the genders "right in her mind," but upon reflection realized she imposed such definitions when none were actually given. The viewer might assign masculine to WALL-E because he's the protagonist, the worker, the boxy one, the one with a manly acronym, because he's got Keaton's deadpan and Chaplin's romantic tramp elegance or because he's the one with the view, the gaze through which we see the world. Still he's not macho, loves musicals, and possesses runaway emotions. Indeed he tends toward sentimentality and quakes in his treads at the display of blockbuster explosive action. Hmm. A queer robot.

EVE, an Extraterrestrial Vegetation Evaluator, has got to be a girl. She's the sight, the object of WALL-E's loving gaze. She's the round one with the girlie acronym and the fashionable blaster. When she appears, WALL-E, who knows love from his favorite video musical, falls for "her" at first sight. Hard. And with desire, he comes to know loneliness. After seven hundred years in paradise lost, finally, someone to share his life, his insights, his treasures with. But alas, beautiful, sleek EVE is more advanced, more powerful than WALL-E, and lethal. Smooth as a bullet and capable of lyrical air ballet, she is a marvel of progress. Watching her dance in the air, Earth-bound WALL-E longs to connect, to take hold of EVE's "hand"—an appendage that is also a gun. No, a missile launcher. Unsentimental, ambitious, and violent. Another queer robot.

In a perfect romantic comedy set-up, when EVE first notices WALL-E she shoots at him and then ignores the shivering hunk of junk as she pursues her "directive." We ache and root for WALL-E as he courts EVE. Despite her destructive power and singled-minded focus, WALL-E finally gets her to his humble abode. "Dancing," EVE could destroy the flimsy storage-unit, but when she giggles her eye-analogues slant to the diagonal and her machine voice is high and sweet. What's not to love? Gender confusion be damned, we love them both. WALL-E and EVE roll/glide along gender boundaries demonstrating the plasticity of that social/biological definition when applied to any of us in our varying degrees of (post-) humanity. EVE and WALL-E's amorous and heroic relationship in the midst of devastating apocalypse and despite rigid robot design is the thrill and delight of the movie.

WALL-E is a meditation on what it means to be human, here and now, as we continue to live in the shock waves of colonialism.

No? Wait, what movie were you watching?

In *Discourse on Colonialism*, Aimé Césaire writes:

> A civilization that proves incapable of solving the problems it creates is a decadent civilization.
> A civilization that chooses to close its eyes to its most crucial problems is a stricken civilization.
> A civilization that uses its principles for trickery and deceit is a dying civilization. (1972 [1955], 9)

Robots are ur-figures in the sf&f landscape. Artists living in the new machine age, in the scientific century, imagined/created artificial humans as they grappled with the implications of colonialist imperialism and predatory capitalism. These modern artists asked: Who are we that stand now against nature, against the savage? Are we rational beings, wizards of science besting God, or genocidal barbarians, or what?

Frankenstein's monster was a staple of the nineteenth century stage. Action-adventure melodrama, the dominant popular form, embraced titillating tales of quasi-human others.[1] Shelley's novel inspired nearly a hundred stage adaptations and audiences were most familiar with the story through these action/adventure melodrama versions.[2] Obedient perfect servants or deadly creations of arrogant scientists and mystics, these popular monsters migrated easily from the stage to silent film. Edison made the first *Frankenstein* film in 1910. Paul Wegener directed his first *Der Golem* in 1915. As satire, folklore, and gothic melodrama encountered realism, suspension

1 *The Octoroon* (1859) by Dion Boucicault, for example, featured freakish sub-humans (white looking black lady, savage Indian), the wonders of new technology (photography), explosions, murder, and chase scenes critical to the plot. Boucicault's realist melodramas defined late nineteenth century American drama and set the tone for film melodrama.

2 See *Gothic Images of Race in Nineteenth-Century Britain* by Howard L. Malchow, 33-38.

of disbelief gave way to credible fantastic worlds, past, present, or future.

Theatrical realism was/is a set of conventions that offers "the illusion of the real." In the mid to late nineteenth century, actors began acting *as if they were in real life*, not on a stage, as if they lived behind an invisible fourth wall. In this illusion, the audience is no longer present to the artistic event—no more direct address, asides, dying twice for a second round of applause. In Realism, the audience gazes on a presentation of objective reality; the world as it is, not as it is seen. Realist characters make sense not simply as stage metaphors, but as people in real life. They have consistent motivation, intention, action. Realist plots often present a linear, cause and effect relation to actions, events, character decisions, and outcomes. Thus dramas are created that are as authentic, as real as reality. Realism posits an omnipotent, God's eye view of truth and then presents that truth as a discovery of what is real, not as a construction of what is real.

Audiences of realism didn't "suspend disbelief," but took even a fantastical world as an alternate world, different from ours but not the product of an individual imagination. Realism on page and stage helps to birth the conceits and artist/audience contracts of sf&f. Ironically, anti-realism is also a midwife. The Futurists, Dadaists, Expressionists, Surrealists rebelled against the illusionist premise of Realism and against its objective, absolute point of view. Truth for the Anti-realists was multiple and subjective, was Picasso and Braque, was a fractured nude descending an infinity of stairwells. To break the illusionary spell of Realism, Antirealists sought a dramaturgy of estrangement.

Antirealist playwright, novelist, and essayist Karel Čapek created an alternate world with a twist and introduced "robots" in his 1921 Expressionist play *RUR* or *Rossum's Universal Robots* (*Rossumovi Univerzální Roboti*). In an early scene, Helena Glory, a member of an organization that supports robot equality, has come to inspect the RUR factory and liberate the human-like workers. These cheap labor machines are androids who, like Blade Runners, Terminators, or Cylons, can and do pass for human. Helena fears robots are being treated worse than "Red Indians" or working class Europeans. Amused by her stabs at robot-solidarity, Domain, general manager for RUR, defines robots for her, but also defines the ideal human worker.

> Domain: But a working machine must not want to play the fiddle, must not feel happy, must not do a whole lot of other things. A petrol motor must not have tassels or ornaments, Miss Glory. And to manufacture artificial workers is the same thing as to manufacture motors. The process must be the simplest, and the product of the best from a practical point of view. What sort of worker do you think is the best from a practical point of view?
>
> Helena: The best? Perhaps the one who is the most honest and hard-working.
>
> Domain: No, the cheapest. The one whose needs are the smallest. Young Rossum invented a worker with the minimum amount of requirements. He had to simplify him. He rejected everything that did not contribute directly to the progress of work. In his way he rejected everything that makes man more expensive. In fact, he rejected man and made the Robot. My dear Miss Glory, the Robots are not people. Mechanically they are more perfect than we are, they have an enormously developed intelligence, but they have no soul. Have you ever seen what a Robot looks like inside?
>
> Helena: Good gracious, no!
>
> Domain: Very neat, very simple. Really a beautiful piece of work. Not much in it, but everything in flawless order. The product of an engineer is technically at a higher pitch of perfection than a product of nature.
>
> Helena: Man is supposed to be the product of nature.
>
> Domain: So much the worse. Nature hasn't the least notion of modern engineering. (1961, 9)

Expressionist Čapek and many other early twentieth century Antirealists were horrified by the brutal tactics of colonialism abroad and capitalism at home.[3] Politicians, philosophers, writers,

3 Of course some Antirealists were Fascists seeking to overthrow old regimes and usher in modernity with violence if necessary. Josef Čapek, Karel's brother and collaborator, was a Cubist painter and wrote essay/manifestos championing the art of the unconscious, the art of children

and captains of industry urged the Europeanization of the world and the mechanization of work. Manifest Destiny! Realism in the theatre supported the status quo and offered the comforting illusion that Europe's superiority in all things gave them dominion over the land and over the bodies and spirits of inferior races, classes. (*As man's superiority gives him dominion over women's bodies.*) After WWI, Fascists in Germany were poised to practice colonialist tactics honed in Asia, Africa, and the Americas on Europe. Mesmerized by realism, European and American audiences were complacent in the face of brutality and destruction.

In *RUR,* Čapek imagines the ultimate mechanization of work—humanlike machines who are cheaper, stronger, and more efficient than humans. Without messy emotions and complicated motives, robots are perfect slaves. Unlike working class Europeans and cheeky savages from every dark continent, robots should not rebel. By design, they know their place and stick to it. (WALL-E and EVE are bad robots!)

RUR's Helena doesn't understand what place "female" robots have.

> Helena: Perhaps it's silly of me, but—why do you manufacture female Robots, when—when—
>
> Domain: When—hm—sex means nothing to them? (27)

Domain explains that it's a convenience, what people expect for certain types of workers, but nobody asks why have male robots when sex means nothing to them. Is gender superfluous without sexuality, or just women, or is the default always male?

Things don't go as planned at RUR. The supposed goal is to replace human workers with robots and offer humanity a work-free utopia, but some robots are modified to be more humanlike, i.e., they are given emotional interiors and subsequently rebel. These robots incite the others to destroy their useless, inferior human oppressors and claim the world for themselves. Human genocide is rationalized and justified by the logic of colonialism that Robots have learned from their human creators. As superior robots kill off inferior humans and take over the world, Domain thinks to manufacture "ethnic" robots who wouldn't be able to communicate and would hate and fight each

and savages who were still in touch with what civilized man had abandoned or lost.

other. This "ethnic" solution comes too late and humans are killed off (57). Approaching his fantastical alternate world realistically, Čapek hoped to embrace and shatter the mesmerizing illusion of realism. *RUR*'s fantastical world was a logical extension of Čapek's present, a realistic WHAT IF.

Film director Fritz Lang and screenwriter Thea von Harbou attempted a similar project with the 1927 Expressionist SF classic *Metropolis.*[4] The workers in *Metropolis* are extensions of the city's mighty heart-machine, laboring to allow the elite a life of decadent leisure. Machines haven't replaced workers, but engulfed them. Lang and von Harbou's vision of mechanistic mobs advancing in lock step to the elevator before descending into the bowels of the machine is still stunning and horrific. Once at their stations, the workers do a danse macabre with the machine, moving as gears and levers. Little more than automatons, these are not Haraway cyborgs redefining social, technological, and biological relations. Yet if they collapse at their stations, the machine spirals out of control and all hell breaks loose in the city above. Dehumanization of the workers powers the Metropolis.

The *Maschinenmensch*[5] or robot in *Metropolis* is a violent blond female who drives rich men wild with erotic dancing and urges poor men to destructive anarchy with irrational rhetoric. A mad scientist has stolen a good woman's form to clothe/disguise his soulless *Maschinenmensch* or perhaps to reveal the hideous core everywoman that torments men. In either case, the conceits of the film are overtly metaphorical. Film's realist premise—what is on screen is authentic reality captured by technology; what is on stage space is metaphorical—affords *Metropolis's* fantastic stylized story strong realist grounding.

Race, class, gender, and sexuality "taint" robots right at the start. From Čapek's *RUR* and Lang's *Metropolis,* antirealist theatre and film artists and their audiences have been fascinated, obsessed, possessed by these marvelous mechanical beings. Robots are never

4 Lang and von Harbou wrote the script in 1924. Von Harbou wrote a novelization in 1926.

5 *Der Maschinenmensch* frequently translated as machine man could be better translated as machine person. Mensch does not equal Mann in German. Mensch leaves the gender open.

quite human, but close enough to offer humans a thrill of terror and joy as we contemplate the distance that separates us and the space we inhabit simultaneously.

Frequently mass-produced, Robots are objects created within a culture but without specific cultural identity. A product of generic formulas and blueprints, not of particular histories, Robots should be unfettered by gender, race, ethnicity, sexuality, etc. Robot bodies should not force identification with biological imperatives, a specific cultural past, stereotypical expectations, or social power. Yet invariably as in *RUR* and *Metropolis*, robots are/become embodied subjects of history and agents of change.

WALL-E is a lush addition to the myth and lore of the Robot. An adventure/romance/ apocalyptic film focused on sentient machines, emotional mechanical monsters, frightful, adorable OTHERS, *WALL-E* appeals to all ages as it challenges us to consider what it means to be human.

Earth as the trashed, exhausted colony of Buy N Large Inc. abandoned by its consumer elite is such a familiar sf&f trope, has become so uncontroversial, so harmless, it is the setting for a children's/ family animated film from Pixar/Disney. Reviewer James Berardinelli contends that "the old-school ecological message of what a consumption-based society can do to a planet when pollution runs unchecked" does not spoil its "comedic aptitude."[6] Old school? I missed when we graduated from ecology high. Yet Robert Walonsky of the *Village Voice* also declares context is beside the point: "*WALL-E* will not be remembered by children—or the adults for whom *WALL-E* is really intended—for its tsk-tsking environmental policy or its Naomi Klein polemics. Rather, you'll adore it because of a cuddly, lonely little robot who breaks your beeping heart."

Wow.

I love it when critics decide who I am and predict what I'll do, forget, ignore.

Sets my mind on fire.

I wonder, is the critic afraid I'll have my own relationship to the film?

---

6 In his ReelViews.net review.

Is he worried that ten-year-olds are reading Naomi Klein's *No Logo: Taking Aim at the Brand Bullies* and won't accept his *Village Voice* cred?

Berardinelli, Walonsky, and other critics[7] argue that an overt political agenda or "message" on the part of the filmmakers doesn't tarnish the artistic achievement of the film. Despite raising "big" or "serious" issues, *WALL-E* magically, brilliantly manages to avoid "a scolding, self-satisfied lecture."[8] Indeed it can pass for decontextualized, ahistorical entertainment.

The shared ideological assumptions of these critics are significant. For them, and by implication for their readership, a visible agenda makes for bad art. *Ars est celare artem*—the nature of art is to conceal, as Ovid said. Artists should craft their work not to expose its artifice, its intentions or formal magic. Secondly, popular artists are on dangerous ground when they critique the institutions and ideologies that support and produce them. As the *New York Times* reviewer A.O. Scott says of *WALL-E*'s writer/director, "Mr. Stanton shows his awareness of the contradictions inherent in using the medium of popular cinema to advance a critique of corporate consumer culture." Besides running the risk of hitting us over the head with a MESSAGE, Mr. Stanton risks being accused of posturing resistance or revolution, making a cynical nod to a green Zeitgeist, but ultimately favoring the ruling corporate consumer ideology—anything less is potentially self-destructive at the box office.

Or is it?

As in *RUR* and *Metropolis*, I believe Mr. Stanton and his creative team use *Maschinenenmenschen* to conceal and reveal. Moreover, the dystopic setting of the film may be uncontroversial but it is not insignificant, irrelevant, or trivial. We don't have to suffer the guilt that might come up if WALL-E were a Chinese coolie, African American slave, Cherokee noble savage, or Indian Untouchable slaving in the trash heaps of his people's once verdant landscape. EVE isn't the technocratic European, Africa, or Asian beauty wiped clean of her ethnicity, betraying her people, her gender, serving the masters in

7 Peter Travers in *Rolling Stone*, Ed Gonzalez in *Slant Magazine*, Stephanie Zacharek at *Salon.com* for example. Gonzalez even uses tsk-tsking as a verb like Walonski.

8 A. O. Scott in the *New York Times.*

exchange for fancy gadgets, house servant privileges, and the illusion of power. Still, this film isn't just any cute, cuddly robot romance in nowhere land.

As comedy, *WALL-E* depends on its various audiences' thorough familiarity with postcolonial, late capitalist tropes and references. The fun of the film is in the ironic twists on the Happy Idea, the Magic If of global capitalists destroying Earth and then instead of sticking around to clean up the mess, shuttling passive consumers off to the stars and leaving uncomplaining robots behind to do the dirty work. We don't need Naomi Klein to provide an ideological context for this cinematic parable. Audience members can draw on their own experiences including a wealth of SF & F fiction, cinema, and plays to develop their plausible theory for humanity's acquiescence to the Buy N Large disaster.

We get the joke.

Even though we may not act like it, we know the Earth is a limited resource. No grand evil here, but causal, banal actions by good people propel us toward disaster.[9]

WALL-E's success is not in spite of its political grounding, but because of its eloquent grasp of our analogous position as robotic widgets in a trash landscape dreaming of the stars. Like WALL-E, we long for singing and dancing, beauty, adventure, and love, as we stack cubes of empty purchases that didn't get us to the heaven happiness promised in the ads.[10] We are or want to be the robots "revolutionized" by love. We are all EVEs, lovers of life, the robots who nurture a creative spark, who, given a chance, will save the planet we still cherish.

Mr. Stanton (et al.) is speaking to our desire, not lecturing us on our evil nature.

Facing barbarism in Nazi-Germany, Antirealist playwright and dramatic theorist Bertolt Brecht wrote his famous essay/manifesto, "*Fünf Schwierigkeiten beim Schreiben der Wahrheit*," or, "Five Difficul-

9 On NPR as I write, California farmers are incensed that the government is "giving the water to the fish" rather than allowing them to pump the estuary dry for irrigation.

10 Anecdote: A young man complained to me that he was terribly disappointed at the narrative he was living. He wanted real life to be as fascinating and thrilling as a video game or an action adventure film.

ties in Writing the Truth." To struggle against lies and ignorance and write the truth, Brecht said artists needed at least:

> The *courage* to tell the truth although it is everywhere denied;
> The *ability* or *cleverness* to recognize truth although it is everywhere concealed;
> The *artistry* to wield truth as a weapon;
> The *judgment* to choose those who might make effective use of truth;
> The *cunning* to spread truth among such folks.[11]

Brecht saw truth-telling as a tall order for artists living under Fascism, but also considered it a problem for those living in the land of the free and the home of the brave.[12] For Brecht, popular culture was the most appropriate medium for truth telling and the artist's major formal tool for spreading truth was *der Verfremdungseffekt*—the distancing, alienation effect. Books have been written on this concept with much fussing and cussing.[13] Here is my subjective hit: To tell the truth in the midst of powerful ideological fantasies, storytellers should use a dramaturgy of estrangement, should transpose "difficult" familiar truth to distant, unfamiliar story-worlds where even defensive audiences might respond to it.

The mere mention of the persistence of colonial, imperial relations is enough to make some folks feel guilty, feel lectured, feel attacked; indeed simply to decenter the dominant group and focus the narrative on some "other" feels like a sermon, a threat, and spoils the

---

11 English translations by author.
Wer heute die Lüge und die Unwissenheit bekämpfen und die Wahrheit schreiben will, hat zumindest fünf Schwierigkeiten zu überwinden.
Er muss den Mut haben, die Wahrheit zu schreiben, obwohl sie allenthalben unterdrückt wird; die Klugheit, sie zu erkennen, obwohl sie allenthalben verhüllt wird; die Kunst, sie handhabbar zu machen als eine Waffe; das Urteil, jene auszuwählen, in deren Händen sie wirksam wird; die List sie unter diesen zu verbreiten. (74)

12 Diese Schwierigkeiten sind gross für die unter dem Faschismus Schreibenden, sie bestehen aber auch für die, welche verjagt wurden oder geflohen sind, ja sogar für solche, die in den Ländern der bürgerlichen Freiheit schreiben. (74)

13 See *Theatre of the Oppressed* by Augusto Boal for an interesting investigation of Brecht's Epic Theatre.

escapist fun. Ovid saw the artist's challenge in crafting an invisible artifice where an audience might lose themselves. Brecht challenges the artist to make the artifice of society visible, to reveal what hides in the open. In a popular detective story or entertaining sf children's film, the audience should find itself.

Rebutting Naomi Klein's *No Logo, The Economist* makes these arguments. One—advertising is not successful at manipulating consumers. Proof? A: Nescafe has lost ground to Starbucks as tastes change. B: Young people have all taken marketing; they're wise to the game. Argument #2—the poor benighted folks of undeveloped third world countries all want our brands, our way of life. Ergo branding and globalization is good. Granted advertising and PR manipulate, but lots of people, not just benighted poor folks, enjoy that (2001, 26-28).

Wow.

That the colonized or disenfranchised should lust after the accoutrements and decorations of power says nothing about the intrinsic value of the things sought and everything about the power relations of the social world that endow the objects with serious *juju*. Whether it's Nescafe or Starbucks, Coke or Pepsi, we seek the narrative possibilities that come with consuming these product/fetishes. Consumers may shift allegiance but they continue to believe buying will make you happy. Even if we know it's a lie, we keep on buying, like the Blob people on Buy N Large's spacecraft. They are all different colors—brown, yellow, and pink blob people but only one consumer culture has survived. A cargo-culture for all of us natives who relate through the things we buy, not the experiences we make together, who all speak logo language, not the poetry of our experience. No more singing and dancing, no more face time, just screen contact as Buy N Large programs kiddie blobs with their consumer objectives. Seven hundred years into our future, race, gender, sexuality, ethnicity are irrelevant, but this is no cyborg utopia. Humanity has become passive pod people—consumer appendages to the corporation, less "human" than the queer robots. The empire operates from within.

WALL-E is about the sacred, is about the magic of being alive. WALL-E and EVE are embodied spirits, endowed with the creative spark and the perceptual capacity to make meaning out of nothing. Through experience, WALL-E and EVE change and are changed by their world. WALL-E sees beauty between the stars, is enchanted by EVE's eloquent grace and lethal power. WALL-E makes art to inspire EVE and cares for her when she is dormant, suffering lightning strikes to keep her company and shelter her from rain. EVE, seeing what WALL-E does, is willing to redefine her directive. With their humble scraps of universal divinity, WALL-E and EVE cause a chain reaction of profound change in the robots and people they meet. Experiences, connections, and relationships, not things, prove precious, revolutionary.

After WALL-E has been electrocuted and crushed in order to help EVE fulfill her directive of finding life on Earth and returning people to their home planet, it seems he will not be able to enjoy the new world that is coming. Frantic, EVE finds spare parts and puts him back together, but WALL-E does not recognize himself or her. Without his memory, his collection of particular experiences, he is nobody. EVE offers him the treasures he once gathered and shared with her. She offers him *Hello Dolly*. He stuffs these now meaningless things into his tummy, compresses them into a cube, and rolls away from EVE and his former home. In saving the world, WALL-E has lost himself.

A desperate moment, hopeless! But EVE takes his hand, finally. Like the once blind girl clutching tramp Chaplin's hand in the end of *City Lights*, saying "you?" WALL-E remembers who he is and who he can be. Body memory, not things, not a memory board of directives restores his spirit. Physical connection calls him back to the WALL-E that EVE and we love.

Romance is revolutionary. Despair turns to triumph as the humans wobble off the spacecraft to a planet where pizza doesn't grow on trees.

Works Cited

Berardinelli, James. "*Wall-E* World" ReelThoughts: November 19, 2008. ReelViews.net. http://www.reelviews.net/php_review_template.php?identifier=1153.

Boal, Augusto. *Theatre of the Oppressed*. London: Pluto Press, 1979.

Bornstein, Kate. *Blog for Teens, Freaks and Other Outlaws.* http://katebornstein.typepad.com/kate_bornsteins_blog/2008/07/walle-a-butchfe.html.

Boucicault, Dion. *The Octoroon.* (original,1859) Available online: http://library.marist.edu/diglib/english/americanliterature/19c-20c%20play%20archive/octoroon-index.htm.

Brecht, Bertolt: "Fünf Schwierigkeiten beim Schreiben der Wahrheit" in *Werke. Große kommentierte Berliner und Frankfurter Ausgabe*, hrsg. von Werner Hecht, Jan Knopf, Werner Mittenzwei und Klaus-Detlev Müller. Band 22.1, Berlin und Weimar 1993, pp. 74–90.

Čapek, Karel and Čapek, Josef. R.U.R. and The Insect Play. Translated by P. Selver and adapted for the English stage by Nigel Playfair. Oxford; New York: Oxford University Press, 1961.

Césaire, Aimé. *Discourse on Colonialism.* (translation, Joan Pinkham). Monthly Review Press, 1972 (original publication 1955).

Ebert, Roger. http://rogerebert.suntimes.com/apps/pbcs.dll/article?AID=/20080626/REVIEWS/963071290/1023.

Haraway, Donna. "A Cyborg Manifesto: Science, Technology, and Socialist-Feminism in the Late Twentieth Century," in *Simians, Cyborgs and Women: The Reinvention of Nature.* New York: Routledge, 1991, pp.149-181.

Klein, Naomi. *No Logo: Taking Aim at the Brand Bullies.* Toronto: Knopf Canada, 2000.

Malchow, Howard L. *Gothic Images of Race in Nineteenth-Century Britain.* Stanford, CA: Stanford University Press, 1996.

Scott, A. O. *New York Times.* http://movies.nytimes.com/2008/06/27/movies/27wall.html.

Walonsky, Robert. *Village Voice.* http://www.villagevoice.com/2008-06-24/film/wall-e-robots-in-love/.

"Who's wearing the trousers?" Economist 360.8238 (08 Sept. 2001): 26-28.

Andrea Hairston is Artistic Director of Chrysalis Theatre and a Professor at Smith College. Her novel, *Mindscape,* won the 2006 Parallax award from the Carl Brandon Society and was shortlisted for the Phillip K Dick and Tiptree Awards. "Griots of the Galaxy," appears in *So Long Been Dreaming*. An essay, "Octavia Butler—PraiseSong to a Prophetic Artist," appears in *Daughters of Earth.*

We Are the Apes Who Pray: WisCon Panel Report

Stef Maruch

> Panel description: To explore the evolution and purpose of the supernatural worldview (in all its forms) as purely a matter of human invention. As an atheist, it is often challenging to foster an uncompromised discussion of religion and spirituality without bowing to the social pressure to "respect" or treat "seriously" beliefs and opinions which, ultimately, have no basis in scientific fact. Beginning with the acknowledgement that human beings are, without exception, products of biological evolution, how do we move forward to discuss religion and belief for what they are: neurological, anthropological, psychological, and sociological aspects of the human condition whose true value rests in what they reveal about us as apes who pray?
>
> Panelists: Erin Cashier, Catherine Anne Crowe, Janet M. Lafler, Keith R. Watson
> Moderator: Richard F. Dutcher

This report includes some useful/important things that were said on the panel. Errors are mine.

- Everyone on the panel was an atheist or agnostic.
- There are many kinds of atheism.
- Changes in government in the nineteenth and twentieth centuries—moving away from the "parish" as a government entity—made it possible to be "out" as an atheist. (I'm not sure which countries this applies to.)

- Sociology has the concept of habitus, which is your perceptions/beliefs/behaviors or your cultural comfort zone. This is largely made up of things you were taught or things you derived from your existing beliefs. There's considerable inertia in what makes up the habitus. Most of this knowledge is based on...my notes say the panelist called it "experience," but I might describe it more as "assumptions based on past experience and a body of knowledge." The example she gave was, "Even though I haven't seen my living room for a day or so, I know there is no bear in my living room."

- Our current experience of living in a world with "competing" philosophies/spheres/ways of life is not the way humans lived for most of human history.

- The question arose whether religious belief has a direct evolutionary advantage. I thought this was an interesting question, but the panelists and audience didn't address the point that human behaviors/traits/tendencies can be influenced by evolution without having a direct evolutionary advantage.

- There is a physiological component to religious experience and many cultures/religions know this and have ways of creating the religious experience. One of the panelists is a diabetic and said that when she has low blood sugar she can get into a state where she feels like she "understands everything." She suggested there might be a connection between this and the fact that many people fast to achieve a religious experience.

- Being part of a group can also affect what a religious experience is like.

- It was claimed that Abrahamic religions (Judaism, Islam, Christianity) are different from other religions because they focus on orthodoxy (you must believe certain things) whereas religions such as Confucianism and Buddhism focus on orthopraxy (you must do certain things). This is an interesting notion, but I don't think it was described very well. First of all, it's not true of Judaism; orthopraxy is at least in some forms of Judaism more important than orthodoxy. Second, insofar as there's a difference between Christianity and Buddhism (I'm using those two religions as examples because I know something about them, having been raised Christian and currently studying Buddhism), I think it's more of a difference of degree than a difference in kind; there's plenty of orthodoxy in Buddhism and there's plenty of orthopraxy in Christianity. I spoke up with a different quibble, though—I said that the focus in Buddhism is on "your behavior will create the correct states of mind" rather than simply on behavior itself.

- How can we create community in the absence of religious organizations? Someone jokingly said "science fiction fandom." But I think that's a real answer, not a joke answer. I think groups of people who gather around a particular interest, whether it be science fiction fandom or the Chicago Cubs, can sometimes develop qualities of community similar to those I have seen in religious organizations. (Not that I claim to have experienced the greatest models of religious community, so I might be talking out of my butt here.)
- Why are people in the US more religious than people in Europe? One theory offered was that a social democratic government, that makes efforts to meet everyone's survival needs, takes over some of the functions of religion. "Nordic" societies came up, and an historical argument was made that because they were small, poor, and neutral, no "extreme income pyramid" developed; in this kind of society people tend to take care of each other. However, no one made the point (which occurred to me just now and I'm not sure it's true, but I've heard it said) that Nordic societies are fairly homogenous ethically. Maybe homogenous societies don't need religion? (But I know of fairly homogenous societies that do have religion, so maybe not.)
- This led into a discussion of how religion has been co-opted by ruling classes, and about cyclical changes in the role of

women in religion. In the West, there have been "waves" of religious "enthusiasm," and in the early stages of such a wave, women are welcomed as preachers, but in the middle stages, women are not allowed to be preachers. The panelist claimed that such a wave is occurring right now in the US/UK.

- People can view political philosophies, even atheist ones, as if they were religious beliefs. Some early communists were very fervent (for example, see the espionage novels of Alan Furst, before World War II), and this explains why so many people "walked into Stalin prisons." (I guess they believed in communism blindly and didn't see the corruption.) Someone suggested that the longer you are devoted to something, the more rigid you can get about it.

- A guy named Randy Thornhill has a theory that religion creates a "protective ingroup." By "protective" he seemed to mean "protective of the immune system." For example, he claims that some US states are more religious because they have more disease. Personally, I might agree there is a protective value to religion, but I'm not sure that this theory gets cause and effect quite right. States that have more actively religious people might have more disease for other reasons. Some of these states have more poverty than average in the US, and that might contribute to disease too.

- Studies have been done where they wired up humans with electrodes and stimulated certain parts of the brain, whereupon the subjects reported "seeing god" or having some kind of spiritual experience. I asked whether any such studies have been done on animals. The panel argued that it wouldn't be possible to study this in animals, because we wouldn't know what the animals were experiencing and wouldn't know which part of the brain to stimulate— "it's easier to find the pleasure center than the god center," I think one of the panelists said. And that's a good point, but I still think it could be tried. I haven't read the studies so I don't know where this religious center is in the human brain, but I wonder whether it's in a part of the brain that other animals also have. I believe that what humans experience as god, other animals experience too, although of course I don't know what they make of the experience. (I joked that when I rub my cat's belly I know she sees god. But of course I don't mean that literally. And besides, I should have said my dog's belly, because I *know* the cat actually thinks that she IS god.)

- Could we "get rid" of religion and get to an "atheist society"? Some people took exception to that wish and said it was anti-freedom or said that we'll never get everyone to agree on a single view of reality. Other people pointed back at the discussion about how the least religious societies are the Northern Europe social democracies.

Our last topic was the relationship between religion and ethics/moral codes. For some reason it got sidetracked onto sociopaths.

Stef Maruch opines about feminism, speculative fiction, fat activism, and more at http://firecat.dreamwidth.org. She lives in the San Francisco Bay Area and hates flying, but WisCon is worth it.

Plastic Personality Surgery

Camille Alexa

I meant to tell you yesterday over coffee
I don't like your latest upgrade.
"Everybody does it," you said, and showed me
the fresh pink perfect tear-shaped pucker beside your eye.

"One for every upgrade," you explained, and stroked the scars.
I counted five.
"I liked you before," I said.
You smiled and added non-caloric sugar to your cup.

I remember you, my sister once;
that so-imperfect child of five and ten and twelve,
scraping knees and breaking things and throwing tantrums—
you were glorious.

That first upgrade was all right, I guess,
though afterward I missed your clumsy stumbles,
the natural ungrace of any gangly, large-boned child;
I have it still.

Operations—upgrades—two and three I hardly noticed
but four left me bereft, left me missing you.
Because they can alter you with science does not mean
you should let them. I miss the smile you used to have:
less plastic.

You smile at me now, and I see again raw holes
in your surgically improved personality.
Give me back my sister, I want to say. *Let her out.*
But she's you five yous ago, so I stay silent.

"I'm popular now, and attractive. I fit in."
You look into my face; I don't look back.
I'd rather close my eyes and see you there inside, instead:
puzzled gaze and nervous laughter and self-conscious flutters
of your hands...

No, truly, you were grand.
I miss you. I try to tell myself your fingers on your tear-drop
scars
stroke there in some echo of your previous, less perfect self,
and
not in conquering triumph over her,
but I fail.

Camille Alexa is Flash Fiction Editor for *Abyss & Apex* and she writes for *The Green Man Review*. Her work appears in *Fantasy Magazine*, *ChiZine*, *Escape Pod*, and various anthologies. Her book, *Push of the Sky* (Hadley Rille, 2009), received a starred review from *Publishers Weekly*. More info at http://camillealexa.wordpress.com.

Octavia Butler's *Wild Seed* and *Kindred*: Black Female Bodies as Sites of Intersection

Erin Ranft

As body theorist Susan Bordo has observed, the control of female bodies—"perhaps the only gender oppression that exercises itself, although to a different degree and in different forms, across age, race, class, and sexual orientation—has to be acknowledged as an amazingly durable and flexible strategy of social control" (1997, 91). Female bodies throughout Western European history have been subjected to scrutiny and oppression based on their difference from the ultimate sites of dominance and patriarchal control: the putative white male body.

As a genre theoretically without boundaries, science fiction offers a space wherein differences intersect and interact, and because of the connection between control and the corporeal, female science fiction authors often infuse their writings with issues related to the physical manifestations of power within a given society or community. Octavia Butler, arguably the first and most prolific African American female author of science fiction,[1] wrote stories exploring how and why Black female bodies become sites for issues of race, gender, class, religion, and numerous other categories. By examining the strengths of intersectionality as a theoretical approach, then applying it to characters within Butler's *Kindred* and *Wild Seed*, I intend

1 Gregory Rutledge (2001) maps the history of African American science fiction. He credits Samuel R. Delany with being the first African American male science fiction author, and Octavia Butler as the first female African American author of science fiction. He admits, though, that stories with elements of science fiction were written before these authors, but Butler and Delany are the first African American writers to intentionally write within the genre (other than potential authors who wrote for the science fiction pulp magazines under pseudonyms).

to illustrate that bodies are integral features when various markers of identity intersect to create a system of domination.

Written only two years before *Kindred* was published, the Combahee River Collective Statement contains perhaps the most salient definition of intersectionality. In 1977, the women of the Collective wrote that the

> most general statement of our politics at the present time would be that we are actively committed to struggling against racial, sexual, heterosexual, and class oppression, and see as our particular task the development of integrated analysis and practice based upon the fact that the major systems of oppression are interlocking. (White 1977, par 1)

The Collective recognized that people sometimes feel a need to compete in what Angie-Marie Hancock calls the "'Oppression Olympics'" (2007, 68), where people rank oppressions according to which group suffers the most. This mentality of placing oppressions on a hierarchy should be overcome because it neglects the ways that categories such as race, gender, class, and sexuality are interconnected. In her article "When Multiplication Doesn't Equal Quick Addition: Examining Intersectionality as a Research Paradigm," Hancock clarifies the two standard approaches to research in identity politics and explains how intersectionality offers an inclusive view of the ways categories interact.

Hancock has theorized the existence of three types of evaluation for the examination of identity categories[2]: the unitary approach, the multiple approach, and finally the intersectional approach. The "*unitary* category serves to bind people into a political group based on a uniform set of expectations" (65) and employs the mindset of solidarity behind a single experience. This approach insinuates that there is a single, unifying category (like gender) that is paramount and independent from all others. The multiple approach implies an autonomous nature between categories of difference rather than viewing the interaction of these categories *and* how certain people can exist in the liminal spaces of these groups. Both unitary and multiple approaches fail to view different categories as pieces of the

2 Hancock's article contains a chart detailing the points of similarity and difference amongst the three approaches (64).

whole. Intersectionality seeks to examine the ways various aspects of identity can affect access to power, justice, education, and so on. As Patricia Hill Collins states,[3] "Rather than examining gender, race, class, and nation as distinctive social hierarchies, intersectionality examines how they mutually construct one another" (1998, 62). Being additionally marked as Black, Black female bodies, even more than white ones, are the sites of multiple categories, including gender and race, and are therefore germane to a discussion of intersectionality.

The main character in Octavia Butler's *Wild Seed*, Anyanwu, appears at first glance to defy the ways that intersectionality can affect a woman's bodily oppression. The novel begins in 1690 with Anyanwu having lived for nearly three hundred years. She is able to shape-shift, metamorphosing into any creature she desires. Living for most of her years in Africa, she has outlived her myriad children and grandchildren, and exists as a feared and respected medicine woman. Only when another powerful entity finds her does Anyanwu consider a different life. Doro, a spirit-being who inhabits whatever body he wishes, seeks out others with remarkable abilities in an effort to create a race of individuals that can live forever. Doro persuades Anyanwu to take part in his endeavor by moving to one of his settlements in New York. Anyanwu learns to fear Doro because, although her bodily abilities seem limitless, Doro's power to possess a body places her life at risk. Because Anyanwu's skills and immortality are so rare, Doro forces her to produce children with various men he has gathered for their talents, including himself. The only time she is safe from the threat of Doro taking her life is when she assumes the shape of an animal. In this way, she escapes his oppression for nearly two centuries, during which time she settles in Louisiana and starts her own family. Without Doro, Anyanwu is free to choose her lovers and keep her children close. Doro relentlessly pursues Anyanwu and, when he finally locates her, continues to use his power to compel her to submit to his desire to create settlements of people with abilities, regardless of the consequences. Only when Anyanwu determines that her own death would be better than an existence riddled with constant fear does Doro realize that he must change. He finally consents to cease his cruel and senseless killings and to allow

3 For further analysis of intersectionality, see McCall (2005), Crenshaw (1991), Collins (2000), and hooks (1984).

individuals to choose their own family futures, rather than forcing them to breed as animals. Doro and Anyanwu live together for many centuries after this agreement is reached[4] and their union leads to a new race of humans with unique skills.

Though *Wild Seed* offers a happy ending for readers, this closing should not diminish the hardships Anyanwu faces under the domination of Doro. According to Ruth Salvaggio, the story contains several "dimensions of Butler's fictive world—not the typical feminist utopia, but a flawed world in which racially and sexually oppressed individuals negotiate their way through a variety of personal and societal barriers" (1984, 78). Anyanwu is undeniably a victim of racial and sexual domination, and these instances of control literally intersect with the body because, though Anyanwu's gift allows her to become any living creature she chooses, ultimately her form, the physical appearance she was born with, is Black and female. She must navigate her material surroundings with the utmost care, especially when she resides in the US South. Her body, while under the control of Doro, is continuously required to produce children. If a child is not gifted, he or she is useless to Doro and a potential target for his body snatching. Anyanwu, though married to Doro's most gifted son, has no choice about whom Doro chooses to breed her with over the years. She is unable to shape-shift while pregnant. Her motherhood—and the emotions and physical connection to her children—also become points of oppression for Doro. He understands how deeply Anyanwu cares for her children. He makes it clear that if she refuses to obey him, he will take the lives of those she loves. Only when Anyanwu decides to take her own life does Doro acquiesce to her demands. In this way, Butler demonstrates that a human woman—like Anyanwu—could use her raced, gendered, mothering body as a means of negotiation and survival. Anyanwu's body begins as the site of Doro's control, but it becomes the instrument that overcomes his oppression.[5]

4 *Wild Seed* (1980) is a prequel to *Patternmaster* (1976), *Mind of My Mind* (1977), and *Survivor* (1978).

5 Butler works towards what Vanessa Dickerson terms the "recovery of the maligned black female body" (2001, 196). Essays contained in Bennett and Dickerson's text seek to examine the reclamation and representation of these bodies.

The issues of bodily oppression also extend to Butler's *Kindred*. The main character, Dana, is transported through time to endure the abuses, humiliations, and effects of slavery. As an "inverse slave narrative" (Steinberg 1984, 467), *Kindred* maps Dana's time traveling experiences from the present time of the novel, 1976, to antebellum Maryland. Dana is ripped through time when a distant relation, Rufus, calls her in his times of need. In her first experience, Dana saves Rufus from drowning only to have a gun pointed at her head for coming near the white boy. Her extreme fear in this situation acts as a catalyst for her journey back to the present where her husband informs her that only a few seconds have passed. Each trip back in time for Dana is accompanied by a dangerous situation for both Rufus and Dana. Against her wishes, she is joined on her second journey by her husband, Kevin. Because Kevin is white, Dana is forced to act the part of his slave, creating a psychological strain on her and on their relationship that Kevin cannot understand. Each time Dana is pulled back in time, Rufus is older and more racist and violent (becoming more like his father). He takes what he wants, including one of his female slaves. Alice is given little choice in the matter, for if she does not submit to the repeated rapes by Rufus, she will suffer a vicious beating. The union between Rufus and Alice will ultimately produce Dana's distant grandmother. Rufus, like Doro, is manipulative and abusive in ways that tempt Dana to allow Rufus to die in more than one instance, but she must endure Rufus's abuses because if he dies, the chain of history will be interrupted and Dana will never be born. On her final trip to the past, Rufus attempts to rape Dana. In this extremely violent scene, Dana kills Rufus and returns to the present without part of her arm. She can never again disconnect from the ways in which she was oppressed and traumatized as a slave.

Unable to control her time travel experiences, Dana struggles to acclimate to her nineteenth century surroundings in an environment where her race, her gender, and her literacy put her body in extreme danger. Butler depicts Dana's body as one that manifests her gender, making sexual assault and rape a constant possibility. She constructs a Black woman in a time when slaves were considered chattels; mere items owned by their masters. Dana is also an educated body, able to read and write, which are abilities that whites consider dangerous for slaves. Her knowledge and her willingness to help other slaves learn to read and write threaten her physical safety. Dana is threatened at gunpoint, brutally beaten, nearly raped twice, and forced into servitude. Like Anyanwu, Dana's body becomes the site of oppression and, ultimately, the only tool to help her escape. Only when her body is in the most danger is she able to return to 1976. Time, place, race, gender, and education all intersect on and within Dana's body, creating a constant state of control and danger for the character. Dana's experience exhibits how, according to Marc Steinberg, "Slavery is a physical condition—it affects the body on a base level; therefore it changes, subtly or corporeally, one's body (as well as one's perception of his or her body)" (473). Dana is physically and intrinsically changed because of her experiences as a slave and that knowledge will forever affect the way she negotiates through the late twentieth century, where violence and racism continue to impact African American female bodies.

Butler leaves Anyanwu and Dana physically safe at the end of their respective stories, but the truth remains that Doro might wake one morning and take Anyanwu's life and body in an instant. Doro is fickle, vengeful, and incredibly powerful. Butler never offers the reader any indication that Anyanwu is completely safe, an authorial gesture that suggests the continuous threat to Black female bodies.[6] Dana travels over one hundred years to return to her home in 1976, but those years have not remedied the potential for bodily violence against Black females. Butler literally rips Dana's arm from her body and leaves it in the past to remind Dana and us that the brutality and subjugation reside in the past *and* the present.

Butler's work "complicates traditional science fiction themes—global and local power struggles, for example—by inflecting such struggles with the implications of gender, ethnic, and class difference" (Mehaffy and Keating 2001, 46). Her work is successful because Butler writes about how these struggles and dangers are connected to the bodies of her characters. Anyanwu, even with a remarkably powerful body, is forced to bear children with multiple men and to endure the possibility of Doro's killing her children. She

6 Bodily danger comes in various forms, some of which are not included in Butler's writing. Margaret Bass (2001) shares her experiences as a heavy Black female body and the struggles stemming from the size of her body.

can never fully escape his tyranny until she threatens to destroy the body he seeks to control. Dana's life is perpetually in peril because of her education, her gender, and her race in a time and location that allows her body to be controlled. The stories offer a cautiously optimistic conclusion as Anyanwu and Dana survive their trials not in spite of their bodies, but because of them. When asked about her inclusion of bodily issues in her work, Butler responded that it is because "the body is all we really know that we have...all we really *know* that we have is the flesh" (quoted in Mehaffy and Keating, 59). Though internal, and to a certain extent, external, identities are fluid, bodies are the places where these aspects of identity will always converge. Bodies are where mind and body are connected. They have historically been sites of oppression, especially for African American females, but Butler offers a glimpse of how Black female bodies can be powerful. Her stories show how the intersections of identity on Black female bodies can in fact free those bodies. Butler writes to awaken her audience to the potential for Black female corporealities to overcome adversity and to indict the white bodies who seek to exert control over Black women. I close with a statement by Audre Lorde, a member of the Combahee River Collective. It reflects how differences, how diversity, can be powerful. In a speech delivered at the Second Sex Conference in 1979, she said:

> Within the interdependency of mutual (nondominant) differences lies that security which enables us to descend into the chaos of knowledge and return with true visions of our future, along with the concomitant power to effect those changes which can bring that future into being. Difference is that raw and powerful connection from which our personal power is forged. (2006, 412)

Butler's stories assert that Black female bodies are the manifestations of these differences, the sites where differences intersect, and that they are the places where oppression can be overthrown.

Works Cited

Bass, Margaret K. "On Being a Fat Black Girl in a Fat-Hating Culture." *Recovering the Black Female Body: Self-Representation by African American Women*. New Brunswick: Rutgers University Press, 2001. 219-30.

Bennett, Michael and Vanessa D. Dickerson, eds. *Recovering the Black Female Body: Self-Representation by African American Women*. New Brunswick: Rutgers University Press, 2001.

Bordo, Susan. "The Body and the Reproduction of Femininity." *Writing on the Body: Female Embodiment and Feminist Theory*. Eds. Katie Conboy, Nadia Medina, and Sarah Stanbury. New York: Columbia University Press, 1997. 90-110.

Butler, Octavia. *Kindred*. Boston: Beacon Press, 2003.

——. *Mind of My Mind*. Garden City, New York: Doubleday, 1977.

——. *Patternmaster*. Garden City, New York: Doubleday, 1976.

——. *Survivor*. Garden City, New York: Doubleday, 1978.

——. *Wild Seed*. New York: Warner Books, 1980.

Collins, Patricia Hill. *Black Feminist Thought: Knowledge, Consciousness and the Politics of Empowerment*. New York: Routledge, 2000.

——. "It's All In the Family: Intersections of Gender, Race, and Nation." *Hypatia* 13.3 (1998): 62-82.

Crenshaw, Kimberlé. "Mapping the Margins: Intersectionality, Identity Politics, and Violence Against Women of Color." *Stanford Law Review* 43.6 (1991): 1241-99.

Dickerson, Vanessa D. "Summoning SomeBody: The Flesh Made Word in Toni Morrison's Fiction." In *Recovering the Black Female Body: Self-Representations by African American Women*. New Brunswick: Rutgers UP, 2001. 195-216.

Hancock, Angie-Marie. "When Multiplication Doesn't Equal Quick Addition: Examining Intersectionality as a Research Paradigm." *Perspectives on Politics* 5.1 (2007): 63-78.

hooks, bell. *Feminist Theory from Margin to Center.* Boston: South End Press, 1984.

Lorde, Audre. "The Master's Tools Will Never Dismantle the Master's House." *The Prentice Hall Anthology of African American Women's Literature*. Ed. Valerie Lee. Upper Saddle River, New Jersey: Prentice Hall, 2006. 412-13.

McCall, Leslie. "The Complexity of Intersectionality." *Signs* 30.3 (2005): 1771-1800.

Mehaffy, Marilyn and AnaLouise Keating. "'Radio Imagination': Octavia Butler on the Poetics of Narrative Embodiment." *MELUS* 26.1 (2001): 45-76.

Rutledge, Gregory E. "Futurist Fiction & Fantasy: The *Racial* Establishment." *Callaloo* 24.1 (2001): 236-52.

Salvaggio, Ruth. "Octavia Butler and the Black Science-Fiction Heroine." *Black American Literature Forum* 18.2 (1984): 78-81.

Steinberg, Marc. "Inverting History in Octavia Butler's Postmodern Slave Narrative." *African American Review* 38.3 (2004): 467-76.

White, Bec, comp. "The Combahee River Collective Statement." April 1977. 28 pars. 09 Sept. 2008 <http://circuitous.org/scraps/combahee.html>.

Erin (Ranft) is currently a doctoral student in the English Department at the University of Texas at San Antonio. Her studies are focused on feminist science fiction by women of color. When she can manage, Erin enjoys spending time with her friends and family, especially her niece, Lilah (a future feminist sci fi fan).

Thank God for the Road

Nancy Jane Moore

We'd planned to make Flagstaff by nightfall, but an hour outside Gallup one of the solar panels on the bus roof started to flap around. Emily and Jo climbed up to check, and discovered several more loose panels.

It was too hot to sit inside while they fixed it, so the rest of us put up sun shades and rested by the road. Not a cloud in the sky; nothing but cactus in any direction, so hot and dry that every time you took a deep breath, moisture dried up all the way down into your lungs.

I sat with Irene, who was teaching me another story.

Irene's our oldest member—over sixty now. But crowds grow real quiet when Irene tells a story.

I'm the youngest by a good ten years: I turn twenty next month. And I'm a guitar picker, not a storyteller. But Irene wants me to learn to tell. It didn't take me long after I joined All Star Traveling Revue to figure out no one ever says no to Irene.

"It rained for days and days," I said, sing-song.

"You have to put more feeling into it," Irene said. "You have to make people know what it feels like when the roof is leaking, and every time you run outside you get soaked to the bone, and you can't imagine ever being dry again."

"I'd like to feel like that."

"No, you wouldn't." But Irene knew what I meant. I've never seen that kind of rain. The places I know get a little drizzle, and everybody's grateful. There are parts of the country where they get too much rain instead of too little, but we never go there. They don't get enough sun to power the bus.

"You've got to make the audience feel wet when you tell that story. You've got to make them shiver, even if it's 97 degrees and hasn't rained in seventeen months."

So I thought back to a time in Austin when they'd had a little rain and we went swimming in Barton Springs. The water was icy cold. It's the only time I remember being wet all over. "They didn't think they'd ever be dry again." I shivered.

"That's more like it."

We got back on the road in early afternoon. "We could stop in the Painted Desert," someone said.

"Yeah," I said. I've never been there.

"Not enough people there to do a show," Jo said. She was driving. "We'll go as long as there's sun. That way we'll make Flag tomorrow."

Sun powers the bus's generator directly. We've got batteries that run a stove, a computer, a few amps, but we haven't got one big enough to run the bus. We don't drive after dark.

I sat up in the front, staring out at the expanse of concrete. The road is crumbling, helped along by cactus and other plants too tough for even drought to kill or cement to stop. An obstacle course. No one ever stays in one lane.

It's desolate here, but not the desperate desolation you get driving east from Denver across the Great Plains. It's not as flat, and things here are the way they were meant to be. The plains weren't supposed to turn into desert, but this place has been bone dry for thousands of years.

The first vehicle we'd seen all day came along about an hour before sunset. Jo was struggling to see in the setting sun. I cupped my hand over my eyes and moved to get a better angle. "Looks like a car."

We stopped. Common courtesy. Though we all checked to make sure we had weapons handy. We're friendly, but we're not fools.

The car held two grown women with three little kids in the back seat. Boxes and suitcases were tied onto everything but the solar panels. The women got out; the kids stayed in the car.

Jo and Irene got off the bus. I tagged along behind. "Where you heading?" Jo asked.

"Central Texas. We hear there's work. Heard anything?"

"We haven't been there since spring," Jo said. It was November. "But they had rain. Might be work."

"You musicians?"

"Musicians, actors, storytellers."

"There a living in that?"

"So long as we travel. Every place needs entertainment."

Irene was making friends with the kids, telling a funny story. I heard giggling.

Jo said, "What do you hear from out west?"

"Things got pretty bad after that last earthquake in LA. Lots of refugees heading everywhere else in California. Jobs dried up."

"Along with everything else," the second woman put in. "Things seem better in Arizona. They said in Flag there was snow in the Grand Canyon."

I've never seen snow. "Oh, Jo, can we go see it?"

"Maybe." Snow is water.

"We almost stayed in Flag. The water wasn't too pricey and there was work. But we got family in Texas."

Jo nodded. "Be careful in New Mexico. They haven't had much rain."

Irene yelled up to the bus windows. Someone threw down a bag. She took out a couple of rag dolls and a little box and gave them to the kids. They squealed, delighted.

Jo frowned—we sell those toys—but no one tells Irene no.

The car went on east. We drove thirty miles and pitched camp near some Anasazi ruins.

"Funny to think," Emily said over dinner, "that highway used to carry thousands of cars at a time. Now we travel all day and only see one other vehicle."

"Thousands of people? That's crazy. There's not that many cars anywhere."

"Look how big it is. Had to be a lot of cars once."

"Emily's right," Irene said. "Used to be everybody had a car, everybody drove this highway."

Irene remembers.

"But oil got pricey and water got pricier, and none of the car makers adapted 'til too late. That's why the only vehicles left are mishmashes like ours.

"Here's the funny thing, though. People have been traveling this pathway for a long time, probably back before the Navajo and the Hopi lived around here. It's the natural path. But this big highway didn't get built until the 1960s. And it's been falling apart pretty much my whole life—I doubt it's had any repair in fifty years. This huge highway was a good road for ninety years, maybe less."

I was surprised. You look at a big road, and you think it must have been there for all time.

"My daddy used to tell a story. Seems when his grampa was a little kid, five years old, his parents moved from Texas to California."

"Was that the Dust Bowl?"

"No, earlier than that, when times were flush—1923, 24. They drove on this very road, except it wasn't even paved back then, much less big and wide.

"They met another car on the road. The folks in it had been in California and were headed back to Texas. Just like us, they stopped and chatted. Nobody else coming; it didn't matter that they blocked the road. Just like now.

"They were driving one of the first cars ordinary folks could buy, a Model T Ford. The future looked bright. With cars, people could go anywhere, live everywhere. Nothing was too far away anymore.

"So people built all these highways and the cities grew to super size. But when the rain stopped falling, the cities died. In another hundred years, this highway will be gone. Though there'll probably be some kind of road. Your kids"—she pointed at me—"might even be driving down it.

"Our grandparents and their grandparents built a major civilization around the automobile. And it lasted a hundred and twenty-five years."

We all got quiet. Even I know a hundred and twenty five years isn't long, not for civilizations.

Finally I said, "So what do we do about it?"

Irene smiled—a big smile, the largest I'd seen in some time. "Why, we start over, child. We try again. It's going to be harder, because we haven't got the resources to be careless this time. You have to pay real attention to build something that'll last longer than a hundred and twenty five years.

"That's why we're out here, telling stories and singing songs, letting everyone know that there is more to life than just surviving. That's our job." She paused. "Getting the rebuilding started, that's your job."

She hooked me, then and there. Youth always knows it can do something better than those who came before. Besides, you don't say no to Irene.

Now, fifty years later, I'm not so arrogant. I know I failed more than I succeeded.

But the road's still here—just two lanes of concrete now. We dug out the rest with pickaxes and a few jackhammers, let the land take it back.

A group in New Mexico sent some old spaceships up to bring spent comets down for water. It's expensive—makes gold look cheap—but it made the Southwest livable again. Nobody wastes it, not this time around. We at least learned that much.

The Southwest is still desert and it's still hot, but people are making lives here again instead of just passing through or withering away. The road is too busy for people to stop and chat in the middle of it, but not so busy that people don't pull off to the side and visit.

You can't have civilization without a road, but you can't let the road take over all of civilization. That's what we aimed for when we rebuilt it.

I think Irene would approve.

Writing "Thank God for the Road"

There's a true story at the heart of this piece of fiction, the one Irene tells about her great-grandfather as a little kid traveling with his parents from Texas to California on a dirt road that would eventually become the storied Route 66 and which in the story is the ruins of Interstate 40. My father tells that story about his childhood move out west. I love the idea of a road so lightly traveled that people going opposite directions could stop in the middle of it and chat awhile as neighbors do in small towns, even on a 1,500 mile trip.

Truth is, I love the road, love taking off to drive a long distance. I've driven in each of the 48 contiguous US states, and I've developed my own list of favorite roads—some classics, like Route 1 up the northern California coast, some less well-known ones, like alternate US 14, which goes through the Big Horn Mountains in northern Wyoming and is only open in the summer.

These roads go through towns, so you have to slow down, but that's okay, because you get to see all those smaller places out there—the ones that are dying out, the ones that are trying to survive by selling antiques and old-fashioned culture, and the ones that have brought in so many big box stores and fast food chains that it's only by referring to your map that you know what state you're in.

These roads also go through some of the most awe-inspiring country you'll ever hope to see, like that other leg of alternate US 14 through the Black Hills in South Dakota.

I'm a sucker for road songs, too. This story borrowed its title from one by Butch Hancock, which you can hear on the Flatlanders album Hills and Valleys. The song and the story don't have anything else in common, except that both express a heartfelt love for the road.

It's a complicated love, because every once in awhile I think about the fact that the dirt road my father went down in the 1920s is now a six lane interstate carrying vast quantities of 75-mile-per-hour traffic. In less than a hundred years we built up this vast network of highways out of those wagon and horse trails. It's probably not sustainable, which is what the story is about.

Though it's also about the importance of roads.

I wrote this story shortly after WisCon in 2009. The ideas started coming together on the way home—Butch's song, Daddy's story, the company of interesting creative people, and driving down the highway.

By the way, US 151, which runs through Iowa and Wisconsin, crossing the Mississippi River at Dubuque, is a nice piece of road. If you're ever driving to WisCon from the west, I recommend it.

Nancy Jane

Nancy Jane Moore is part of the online writers' consortium Book View Café (www.bookviewcafe.com). Her novella *Changeling* is published by Aqueduct Press, and her collection *Conscientious Inconsistencies* is available from PS Publishing. She has studied martial arts for more than thirty years and holds a fourth-degree black belt in Aikido. In a former life, she worked to develop food and housing co-ops and worker-owned businesses.

The Transgressive Woman Warrior

as presented by Valerie Guyant and Kate Fruend

[We chose to work within the academic framework but not present academic papers per se. Our apologies to anyone whose comments are not represented here, but we didn't tape the session and have also had to shorten the presentation for space allotment. We know that we discussed a number of issues and works of fiction not included herein, but hope that we managed to capture the gist of the discussion.]

Valerie: Thank you all for coming. I am **Valerie** Guyant and my fellow panelist is **Kate** Fruend. Rather than reading papers, we are going to discuss different sides of the complex issue of the woman warrior who transgresses. We welcome comments and suggestions, in a round table format, as we go along. Please don't feel as if you need to wait until the end.

Kate: We want to stress that we are not looking at real-world female warriors or soldiers, in an effort to limit the scope of the discussion today. Real-world examples of transgressive woman warriors certainly exist, as evidenced by historical figures such as Joan of Arc, but we will leave that discussion for another panel on another day. For today we are interested in the ways that female warriors in the worlds of literature and film can be used as a means of social commentary and as examples of how to live better or different lives, partly because they reflect qualities we want to have, or those we already see in ourselves, in a more dynamic way.

Valerie: We are working from a firm belief that an investigation of transgressive women requires what Joss Whedon labeled the "Bring Your Own Subtext" principle (quoted in Larbalestier 2002, 228). He asserts that authorial intent is not the only, or even the best, explanation for what occurs in a work. Kate or I may view a particular action as transgressive in some way, and many of you may disagree; that's what makes the conversation interesting.

Kate: Keep in mind that we are referring to women who transgress against OUR society's gender expectations, rather than committing some form of moral or legal transgression. That doesn't imply that these women have transgressed against their individual principles. The implication is most often that their transgressions are positive choices in some way.

Valerie: Also, there have been many societies in which women warriors are expected

Kate: The Amazons immediately spring to mind.

Valerie: Right, and for those women, being a warrior was/is not a social transgression, even if we might find such attitudes wrong somehow. Also, there are situations in our own society when we tend to accept a woman as a warrior/soldier, such as when she is protecting her children or seeking revenge for some injustice. These women, while behaving as warriors, are not transgressing patriarchal expectations.

Kate: I would like to point out that when we refer to a "patriarchal society" we are not implying that all men act in a certain way *or* that only men place a "transgressor" label upon these women. We refer to the traditionally instilled values of our society that still cling to the public consciousness.

Valerie: Exactly. Since women who can fight have become rather common in our media, we want to concentrate upon the "just woman warrior" who may use violence to protect the helpless and "right wrongs" in ways that are considered "wrong" somehow.

Kate: Those women who don't follow the rules "society" has established, but what they believe to be morally or ethically "right."

Valerie: Rhonda Wilcox points out, "one of the strengths of the best of these characters is that they are not monolithically virtuous" nor are they morally infallible (2001, x). Their complexity makes them fascinating and allows them to be subversive. Further, Marilyn Farwell suggests that it is possible for the female just warrior to "redesign elements of the viewer's expectations of heroism, stretching [them] to accommodate female agency" (1996, 58). Although Farwell's comment has a limited scope, her point can be applied to reader's expectations, and the "stretching" being asked of us includes accepting new definitions of virtue, ethics, and morality.

Kate: One of the interesting questions, of course, is whether these challenges and disruptions serve as positive examples, whether the women are positive role models.

Valerie: It is certainly fascinating that the first significant influx of tough women into popular media coincided with the height of Second-Wave Feminism in the US. On the surface, such a juxtaposition of social change and popular culture icons would seem to support Farwell's contention. However, Sherrie Inness believes that these early women warriors, such as Charlie's Angels, the Avengers' Emma Peel, and Catwoman, actually "helped to reaffirm stereotypes about the sexuality and femininity of women, attributes that worked to diminish the impact of the women's toughness" (1999, 49). Additionally, most 1960s and 1970s "tough girls" were either following the orders of a man, therefore not really transgressing, or they were the villains. Mixed messages of empowerment and servitude, strength and evil, both confirmed and denied the impact and importance of feminist actions.

Kate: And, as Valerie pointed out while we were prepping, the woman warrior in general, and certainly the just woman warrior, experienced a resurgence in popularity during the 1990s, during the same time that Third-Wave feminism began to gain power. Many current women warriors are positive role models because they subtly address issues of psychological oppression that need to be our primary concerns as we move away from the physical/legal/economic oppressions that Second-Wave feminism strove to overcome. Psychological oppression, while less blatant than physical or legal oppression, is more difficult to identify. As an example of how psychological oppression, transgression, and the woman warrior can weave together an empowering message of identity and individuality, I would like to use Alice from *Resident Evil*, through the lens of Sandra Lee Bartky's theory, which discusses the psychologically oppressive impact of patriarchal power structures on women.

Psychological oppression breaks the spirit of a dominated people, thus rendering them incapable of understanding their oppression. Psychological oppression of women is primarily implemented through stereotyping, cultural expectations, and sexual objectification. Often stereotyped as intuitive, and therefore less rational, women are also sexually objectified, which becomes oppressive when this identity is habitually extended into every area of a woman's experience (Bartky 1990, 52). *Resident Evil* illuminates Bartky's theory on women's psychological oppression through all of these channels, as well as offering methods that women can use to break free from their own psychological oppression.

At the beginning of the movie, Alice wakes up, naked, in the shower with no memories. She walks around the house and looks for clues as to who she is and how she should act. She puts on the clothing laid out on the bed and begins constructing her sense of self from the clues she finds. Symbolically a newborn female child, she is learning how she is supposed to act and who she is supposed to be from the culture and objects around her—a symbolic act of socialization, whereby she socializes herself according to the patriarchal culture in which she finds herself immersed. Most of the cultural objects she bases her identity on place her in a submissive position to a man whom she does not know, especially the wedding picture (of him standing above her), the wedding ring (historically symbolizing his ownership of her), and the dress laid out on the bed (traditional female attire).

Sandra Bartky insists that, "To claim that women are victims of social and cultural domination is to claim all items in said culture, including language, institutions, art, literature and popular culture, are all sexist, or that they all manifest male supremacy. This means that the subordination of women is so pervasive that it appears to be unalterable or natural" (1990, 53). Simply put, "the subordination of women, then, because it is so pervasive...will [if uncontested] appear to be natural—and because natural, unalterable" (55). Alice demonstrates the apparent truth of this concept by accepting the role her environment suggests as if there is no other, internalizing the "natural" personality her cultural cues suggest. Alice's initial behavior is akin to actions women perform daily, even as she is constructing her behaviors. Women have become masters at seeing themselves through the eyes of men and making themselves more appealing based on these expectations; "Subject to the evaluating eye of the male connoisseur, women learn to evaluate themselves first and best. Our identities can no more be kept separate from the appearance of our bodies than they can be kept separate from the shadow-selves of the female stereotype" (55-56). Although Bartky is focusing primarily on obvious grooming rituals in a patriarchal culture, Alice's early behavior exemplifies the ways in which women also subtly mold their behavior to be more appealing to men. Before Alice remembers who she is, she is quiet, meek, and compliant. She follows the men, and although she has a few questions, accepts what they tell her. In many cultures, women are socialized from birth to be quiet and meek, as has been nearly universally true in America until recently. Historically, society as a whole is not surprised when women do not speak up for themselves. Instead, they are as shocked at women demanding rights as the *Resident Evil* audience is when Alice begins fighting.

During the first attack of the zombies, Alice watches, submissive and confused, as the group attempts to kill these zombies, because she doesn't think she has a different option. Later, zombies attack her while she is alone. Without time for anything other than an instinctual reaction, Alice begins to kill the zombies and escapes the room alive. When she kills the first zombie with a kick to his head, Alice is surprised, but quickly adjusts and eventually saves the remaining crew. She sheds the psychologically oppressive personality and behavior that her surroundings initially imposed upon her and accepts her place as a female warrior.

Bartky argues that psychological oppression is extremely harmful for two reasons. First, the person who holds stereotyped beliefs about a group of people cannot understand the needs or rights of individuals within the group (55). Many of us know that there are other options for how to behave as and toward women, but women who are unable to see another option are trapped in a submissive role. Alice shows how pervasive this idea is in our culture. Women are not all naturally submissive, and, as society exalts women who are more powerful and less stereotypical, more women will shed the meek protective cover they are wearing and celebrate the powerful, self-sufficient individuals they can be.

The second reason Bartky considers psychological oppression so dangerous is that, when people begin to believe the stereotyped expectations of themselves, they find it difficult to achieve self-actualization. Our society places a high value on the development of autonomy and moral agency, but sees women as denying their femininity when they become too independent (56). Since traditional female roles and the female stereotype are interwoven (56), Alice's behavior is unimpeded while she is initially in the house, waking up in the shower, discovering she is married, and making herself attractive. It isn't until she attempts to leave the house alone that she is placed under male control. Women, confined to the home or supervised by men, are unable to attain self-actualization. The movie suggests that women already have the ability to reach self-actualization if they are strong enough to fight the zombie-like society that is attempting to keep them acting within certain roles. More importantly, it is only after Alice attains independence that she is able to lead the survivors to safety. Her warrior stance allows her to break free of male control, free of the zombies, and free of social expectations. Psychologically oppressed individuals in the real world can emulate Alice's courage to protest who and what they are expected to be.

Audience member: So is Alice only transgressive because she fights, or is there more to it than that?

Kate: Her willingness to fight is only marginally transgressive. Women who fight are showing up in film and books constantly. It's more about her leading the fight, saving people, and, most importantly, breaking free of the psychological oppression that seeks to confine her.

Audience member: Yeah, about psychological oppression... I would like to go back to your earlier comment that we don't need to worry about physical, legal, or economic oppression of women anymore...

Valerie: I would like to address that issue if I may. I think what we were trying to suggest is not that these other types of oppression no longer exist, but that because of changes in how society now perceives female rights and understands the legal, economic, and physical oppressions that women are forced to endure, a lot of science fiction and fantasy is freer to address issues of psychological and sexual oppression, instead. I'll use the episode "Beer Bad" from *Buffy the Vampire Slayer* as an example. In this particular episode, Buffy deals with the fallout from falling for the "sensitive guy" act perpetrated by Parker in order to convince her to sleep with him. She has not been physically oppressed; she appears to have made this choice on her own. However, analyzing the episode, we discover that Buffy responds to socially ingrained cues that convince her she is at fault. She assumes that she has "done something wrong" or "she wasn't that good" and that is why Parker is ignoring her. That response is an example of psychological oppression at work.

Kate: And that serves as a segue into our discussion of the erotic as a potential form of power that the transgressive woman warrior makes use of. As Audre Lorde mentions in *Sister Outsider*, "the power of the erotic within our lives can give us the energy to pursue genuine change within our world" (1984, 59).

Valerie: Lorde also explains that the erotic functions within each of us in several ways, not just through the sex act (56). She believed that embracing who we are, all that we are, takes power away from masculine, societal expectations and gives it to the individual. It transfers control. Many of the most powerful (and I don't mean physically) women warriors are in touch with the erotic sides of themselves. And yes, sometimes, that may include graphic explorations of their sexuality, such as currently is occurring in the Anita Blake series. However, the interesting aspect of Anita Blake, the reason that I don't believe it is simply "reduced to the pornographic" (59), is that Anita becomes stronger mystically, physically, and psychologically, as she becomes more attuned to her own sexual needs and desires. I see a lot of head shaking in the audience, and I know that many people are frustrated by the direction Hamilton has taken this series; please, just let me explain my thinking, and then we can discuss all the things that bother you.

Anita's sexuality and her mystical powers are interconnected and essential to her character development. As she allows herself to embrace her own desires and act upon them, her metaphysical powers continue to grow. She is the connecting force in a triad of power with the vampire Jean-Claude and Richard, the Ulfric of the local werewolf pack. In a reversal of Terry Castle's patriarchal triangle (1992), the two men are not exchanging a bond *through* Anita; rather each is strengthening a bond *with* Anita. The same is true of her bonds with Nathaniel and Damian, both of whom have developed more strength of character since becoming involved with Anita.

Certainly, our society has traditionally considered female passivity to be the proper response within a relationship, although that response is slowly changing. Socially, any woman who willingly accepts multiple sexual partners, exhibits an aggressive attitude towards sex, or uses sex as a weapon is still considered "abnormal" or evil. That Anita began the series as a sexually chaste woman and is now "guilty" of these behaviors, but is still the protagonist, exemplifies Simone De Beauvoir's view that an honest display of female eroticism "reflects the complexity of the feminine situation" (1953, 372).

Freedom of sexuality and sexual expression may serve as a method of discovering freedom of self and defining one's own power. However, Joanna Russ warns us not to adhere to the traditional belief that, "Sexual behavior and sexual preference are the core of the human personality—or at the very least a faithful barometer...so that sexuality is a fundamental shaper and predicator" (1985, 66). Rather, female sexuality "depends upon the whole experience and situation of the individual" (Beauvoir, 373). It is the whole experience and situation of women's lives that inform and shape them, sexually, emotionally, and intellectually.

Initially, Anita considers her metaphysical ability to animate the dead as a curse or disease. She states numerous times that she has to use her ability or it leaks out unexpectedly, creating "road kill" parades. Her career was not a choice, in her estimation; it was a necessity. She is regularly surprised by her abilities as they manifest. As she becomes less what others expect of her and more what she desires or needs for herself, and begins to accept her diverse physical desires, she gains confidence in her metaphysical abilities and becomes a force that the monsters fear; it's no longer just her willingness to kill that makes her dangerous. Exploring Anita's love life, admitting that it is far from the traditional "accepted" norm, and emphasizing that most of the people in her life understand and appreciate her appetites are empowering specifically because her actions call traditional sex roles in to question.

Audience member: The problem that I have is that it seems like the books are only about sex now. There's no plot; there's no mystery; the reason I started reading them in the first place is because I liked the violence. I need some killing in my Anita stories. If I had more of that, I don't think I'd mind the sex as much. I mean there was one book, and I don't even remember which one anymore, where it seemed like there were 10 pages of actual story and 300 pages of sex.

Audience member: For me, the issue I have is that she doesn't seem to have any control over who she sleeps with. It's not her choice; it's a compulsion. Seems like the books are suggesting that sex is the only way out of any situation.

Audience member: Right, the books themselves have said that she can use anger just as much as she could use sex, yet it always seems that she relies on sex as her only option.

Kate: But the control and the avenues she uses are changing as she gains control. She uses anger more often, she directs and controls the *ardeur* more, and she "has to" have sex less often as long as she willingly feeds her desires rather than refusing to acknowledge them.

Audience member: What's even worse, is that it seems like every time they need to consolidate their power with some other supernatural group, Anita has to have sex with the leader, who of course is always male.

Audience member: It's almost like she has become the temple priestess. Her choices have been taken away from her because she is in league with monsters and she is the sacrifice in order for them to gain power.

Audience member: I find it interesting that everybody is really upset about the idea that Anita sleeps with people in order to gain power. In the real world, we often assume that a woman who rises to power slept her way there, even if it's not true, as if sleeping with someone to get something out of it is automatically a bad thing.

Valerie: I guess one of the things I'm suggesting is that it would be really great if we eventually were able to get past the kind of puritanical belief that using sex automatically makes a woman a bad person. I think it would be great just once if a woman, accused of "sleeping her way to the top," answered "Yes, I did; and I'm OK with that."

Audience member: So, are we actually suggesting that just because she has sex she's transgressive? Is that really all it takes?

Valerie: Certainly not. The fact that she has sex is far less important than the decisions she makes about herself, her relationships, and her power. She transgresses by choosing to maintain relationships with several men, not just by sleeping with them. She transgresses by accepting, even embracing, the idea that her life works best with Nathaniel acting as her "wife" and Micah as a husband. I think it is particularly important to look at Anita's relationship with Dolph, the quintessential patriarchal symbol. As Anita becomes more emotionally independent, Dolph becomes progressively more disappointed and disapproving. And his behavior is considered inappropriate and inexplicable even to others in authority positions. Even Zerbrowski agrees that she is better at her job and happier now than she ever has been.

Kate: I would like to add something regarding why this series is an excellent example of how empowering the representation of a transgressive woman warrior can be. I recently read an interview with Laurell in which she expresses surprise at the number of women who have written her over the years, thanking her for the strength Anita has given them to leave abusive situations. These women think "Anita wouldn't take it," so they refuse to (Levitt 2008). Regardless of how many people seem to feel that Anita's "sleeping around" invalidates the entire series, I would like to express how valuable Anita has been in my own life. As Anita becomes more self-assured and ceases to tolerate certain behavior from the men in her life, I have internalized her strength and have also ceased to tolerate such treatment, including leaving a relationship that was certainly headed towards physical abuse and standing up to my dogmatically Christian family regarding my own life choices. Aided by Anita's choice to believe only parts of her church's beliefs as they apply to her, I have chosen not to live a "Catholic" life. I've also found the strength and self assurance to choose relationships that help me be a better person rather than enabling someone else's desperate desire to control me. "Reading Anita" has freed me, and I'm certainly not the only one. Plus, it's hard for me to believe that this series is the only one that has such an affect on people who needed some form of guidance in order to get out of, or even recognize, the negative aspects of parts of their lives that are holding them back.

Valerie: As much as I would love to sit and talk about Anita Blake for the rest of our time, because it seems like such a loaded topic for our audience, Kate's comment offers a great transition. I would like to suggest that there are a number of women, of whom Anita is one, whose transgressions include their reproductive choices—either being strong, single mothers or choosing not to become mothers. Sarah Conner is one of the most immediate examples. Buffy is another, and the "Kick *ss Moms" panel came up with a long list of female characters who are both warriors and mothers; some of them certainly transgress against social expectations. One of the benefits of these transgressive characters is that they call into question social expectations about women's needs and desires regarding motherhood. Kate mentioned a sense of empathy with Anita that allows her to "transgress" through emulation. While this is a fabulous reaction to a transgressive woman warrior, and certainly a type of social response that makes her valuable, it is important to note how many of these female characters are white, middle class, pretty, young, slim, and blonde, leaving many of us feeling as if we are unable to emulate them because they are so unlike us.

Laura Ng asserts that the absence of boundaries or traditional social constructs allow "transgressive characters on the fringe the ability to explore new ground and construct their own codes" (2001, 110). The problem with so many of these characters being on the fringe is that they are the "other" or the outsider. The most powerful women warriors are rarely "normal" or average, meaning that the girl/woman who looks to them as role models is reaching toward an unattainable goal. Relying upon Edward Said's theories pertaining to Orientalism, Vivian Chin tackles this specific question regarding Buffy, but the same is certainly true of many others (2003). The central question that Chin asks is how the average woman can actually identify with the woman warrior. I would like to add to that the question of how the average man can actually picture someone he knows in that woman warrior role. Can someone from a different ethnic background or a different sexual orientation identify with a young, white woman even if she inhabits an outsider role? If we cannot picture ourselves or those we know in a transgressive role, is it possible for us to believe that those transgressions are feasible in the real world?

Audience member: Realistically, one of the problems we begin to delve into when we start talking about what "types" the media represents, is the question of who determines what we see. For the most part, films play to the lowest common denominator. If the audience is willing to pay to see "hot" women fighting, then the studios are going to give it to them. The same is true with any of the large publishing houses. If we wanna change what they offer us, we have to change what we buy.

Audience member: I know I certainly wouldn't mind seeing or reading the occasional, overweight, but still kick butt, female. Maybe what we need to do is start our own publishing house.

Kate: We could name it The Everywoman Warrior Press. [laughs from the audience]

Valerie: I think essentially what we're trying to say is that the more often we see women that we can identify with behaving in ways that we might either empathize with or want to emulate, the more likely it is that we will work towards changing our society to reflect those behaviors. The woman warriors that we have now just aren't enough.

Kate: Despite the limited demographic offered though, the influx of transgressive woman can lead to a positive social reaction to a fictional representation.

Works Cited

Bartky, Sandra Lee. *Femininity and Domination.* New York and London: Routledge, 1990.

"Beer Bad." *Buffy the Vampire Slayer*. Writ. Tracey Forbes. Dir. David Solomon. WB. 2 Nov 1999. DVD. Mutant Enemy Productions.

Castle, Terry. "Sylvia Townsend Warner and the Counterplot of Lesbian Fiction." In *Sexual Sameness: Textual Difference in Lesbian and Gay Writing*, ed. Joseph Bristow, 128-147. London: Routledge, 1992.

Chin, Vivian. "Buffy? She's Like Me, She's Not Like Me—She's *Rad*." In *Athena's Daughters: Television's New Women Warriors*, eds. Frances H. Early and Kathleen Kennedy, 92-102. Syracuse, NY: Syracuse University Press, 2003.

De Beauvoir, Simone. *The Second Sex*. New York: Knopf, 1953.

Farwell, Marilyn. *Heterosexual Plots and Lesbian Narratives.* New York: Columbia University Press, 1996.

Hamilton, Laurell K. *Black Moon Inn* (Omnibus). New York: Science Fiction Book Club, 1998.

———. *Blood Noir*. New York: Berkeley Books, 2008.

———. *Cerulean Sins*. New York: Berkley Books, 2003.

———. *Club Vampyre*. (Omnibus). New York: Guild America Books, 1997.

———. *Danse Macabre*. New York: Berkley Books, 2005.

———. *Incubus Dreams*. New York: Berkley Books, 2004.

———. *The Laughing Corpse*. New York: Ace Books, 1994.

———. *The Midnight Café*. (Omnibus). New York: Guild America Books, 1997.

———. *Narcissus in Chains*. New York: Berkley Books, 2001.

———. *Obsidian Butterfly*. New York: ACE Books, 2000.

———. *Skin Trade*. New York: Berkley Books, 2009.

Inness, Sherrie. *Tough Girls: Women Warriors and Wonder Women in Popular Culture*. Philadelphia: University of Pennsylvania Press, 1999.

Larbalestier, Justine. "*Buffy's* Mary Sue is Jonathan: *Buffy* Acknowledges the Fans." In *Fighting the Forces: What's at Stake in Buffy the Vampire Slayer*, ed. Rhonda V. Wilcox and David Lavery, 227-238. New York: Rowman and Littlefield, 2002.

Levitt, Aimee. "Mistress of Horror: Nobody Writes Vampire Novels the Way St. Louis' Laurell K. Hamilton Does—and Yes, There's a Lot of Sex." *River Front Times*. 18 Nov 2008. <http: www.riverfronttimes.com>.

Lorde, Audre. "Uses of the Erotic: Erotic as Power." In *Sister Outsider*, 53-59. Trumansburg, NY: The Crossing Press, 1984.

Ng, Laura. "'The Most Powerful Weapon You Have': Warriors and Gender in *La Femme Nikita*." In *Athena's Daughters: Television's New Woman Warriors*, eds. Frances Early and Kathleen Kennedy, 105-118. Syracuse: Syracuse University Press, 2001.

Resident Evil. Dir. Paul Anderson. Perf. Milla Jovovich, Michelle Rodriguez, Eric Mabius, James Purefoy. 2002. DVD. Sony Pictures, 2002.

Russ, Joanna. *Magic Mommas, Trembling Sisters, Puritans and Perverts: Feminist Essays*. Trumansburg, NY: Crossing Press, 1985.

Wilcox, Rhonda V. Foreword: "Out Far or In Deep." *Athena's Daughters: Television's New Woman Warriors*, ed. Frances Early and Kathleen Kennedy, ix-xii. Syracuse: Syracuse University Press, 2001.

Valerie Guyant is a member of the instructional staff at the University of Wisconsin–Eau Claire. She is currently working toward her doctorate through Northern Illinois University in Dekalb, IL, with a dissertation that addresses female characters in vampire fiction. She is married with two budding sf/f enthusiast sons and eagerly awaits the chance to explore all the great novels listed in the response to this presentation.

Katherine Fruend is an undergraduate student at University of Wisconsin–Eau Claire. She is currently looking into graduate school, hoping to research the influences of Romanticism on Speculative Fiction. Kate grew up watching Star Wars with her dad, which is still her favorite although her other favorites are more modern, including the Anita Blake series, Firefly, and Resident Evil.

The Continuing Vision and Revision of the Transgressive Woman Warrior: A Response

Nancy Jane Moore

Emma Peel changed my life. Or rather, the way I remember Emma Peel changed my life. In my memory, Mrs. Peel rescued Steed most of the time. Although she was also very smart, I saw her as the muscle in the team.

People often ask me why I took up martial arts. I usually say it was because I wanted to be able to defend myself. That's true, but it doesn't explain where I got the idea that studying martial arts would make that possible. I've always been a little embarrassed to admit that I got it from watching *The Avengers*, but, in fact, I did.

Emma Peel had studied martial arts—the show was a bit vague about which ones, though both karate and judo were implied—and she could kick ass. She wasn't a superhero; she didn't have magical powers. Rather, her training in Asian martial arts, which emphasize ways a small person can handle a large one, gave her the skills necessary to fight her way out of messy situations. There's irony here: What made Mrs. Peel appear to be a powerful fighter was not actual martial arts skill, but Diana Rigg's consummate skill as an actor. In retrospect, the fighting was laughable, but Rigg made me believe in the power of Emma Peel.

A light dawned: I could learn to do this, too. And if I learned to fight, I wouldn't have to be afraid of men.

Because that's the crux of the matter: Patriarchal[1] society depends on women being afraid of men. Even men who have no power over other men can control women, giving them an outlet for their

1 "Patriarchal" is a word that carries a lot of baggage, but as Valerie L. Guyant and Kate Fruend pointed out in their presentation, it is a useful term to describe "the traditionally instilled values of our society that still cling to the public consciousness."

anger that keeps them from fighting authority. Decent men condemn the abusers, and cherish and protect women, but even they believe women to be fragile creatures in need of protection.

And women believe it. Most women don't think they can take care of themselves. Even over the past forty years, as we have gradually demolished many of the barriers put in front of women, even as we have begun to acknowledge that women—not just the rare exceptional woman—can be powerful athletes and winning trial lawyers, can run large corporations and do brain surgery, can repair cars and install plumbing, women still go in physical fear of men. Where's there's physical fear, there's psychological fear. Combined, they keep women in check.

That's what makes the woman warriors of fiction so powerful and attractive for women: It shows them women who aren't afraid of men and gives them the idea that perhaps they, too, don't have to be afraid. Once women start taking steps to free themselves from fear of men, everything changes. Because there's nothing more transgressive against patriarchal society than women who are not afraid of men.

Let me repeat that: There's nothing more transgressive against patriarchal society than women who are not afraid of men. In an earlier essay (2007, 134) on women and warriorship, I observed, "Once enough women know the basics of self defense, we will no longer be seen automatically as a group of victims, all of us vulnerable to attack on the sole ground of our gender." When women feel safe physically, psychological control loses its power.

Because I was personally drawn to a lifetime of martial arts study by a fictional woman warrior, I chose to attend the presentation on "The Continuing Vision and Revision of the Transgressive Woman Warrior" by Kate Fruend and Valerie L. Guyant at WisCon 33. The program was billed as a debate between the principle that "the transgressive woman warrior is an empowering archetype that transcends gender boundaries" and the opposite argument that "the most powerful of women warriors" are rarely "considered 'normal' or average, meaning that the girl/woman who looks to them as role models is reaching toward an unattainable goal." I was curious, because while I strongly believe both in the positive image of the fictional woman warrior and the ability of women to develop real fighting skill, I also find many of the fictional women heroes less than compelling. Some—like their male counterparts—are strong due to powerful magic that no one can possibly imitate. Some are frankly ludicrous (*Charlie's Angels* comes to mind), completely unbelievable warriors that no one would ever take seriously. And, of course, there's the sex appeal angle.

In fact, the presentation wasn't a debate; it quickly became clear that both Fruend and Guyant share my attitude that the woman warrior in fiction is, on the whole, an empowering figure for women, though they are critical of some of the images presented. Over the course of the presentation, they made several points that are worthy of more discussion.

One thing they emphasized early on: The transgressive woman warrior is fighting for a reason, not just fighting for herself. That is, she is a just warrior. Certainly, in fiction, women warriors are generally on the side of truth and justice (or, at least, what they perceive to be the side of truth and justice). However, the same could be said of most male warriors in fiction. I think our appetite for the just warrior in stories is probably something that crosses gender lines.

But Fruend and Guyant went on to make another observation, one I found both fascinating and provocative: They asserted that a female just warrior is one capable of disrupting the male ideal of the just warrior. That implies, at the very least, that women's ideas on justice might differ markedly from those of men. Unfortunately, this particular point was not discussed in any detail. It's a good starting point for another presentation.

I was also intrigued by their discussion of the theories of Sandra Bartky, particularly her ideas on psychological oppression. While addressing physical fear can undercut a lot of psychological damage, the fact of sexual attraction and desire between men and women can open the door to other kinds of psychological manipulation. In my notes, I have a paraphrase of one idea Fruend and Guyant attributed to Bartky: If a woman is made to be aware of her body at all times, she can never be anything else. Again, this is a provocative statement worthy of greater discussion.

However, I was disappointed by the focus on Laurell Hamilton's Anita Blake books. In the first place, while a woman taking control of her sexuality is certainly a transgressive act in patriarchal culture, it is not a necessary subset of warriorship. Stories showing tough women as sexually desirable (and not simply because they are portrayed by sexy actresses lusted after by young men) are a worthwhile antidote to the psychological manipulation of "no man will fall in love with a fighting woman," but warriorship is a much broader topic than that.

Secondly, I don't find the sexual escapades in the Anita Blake stories all that transgressive. Given that they revolve around sex with a variety of supernatural beings, they strike me as simply a speculative fiction version of a woman having sex with "bad boys." Yes, that breaks some taboos, but it's hardly new ground. Plus I found that the tough warrior side of Anita Blake got lost in the transition of the books from a focus on her skill at fighting vampires to her sexual relationships.

I got bored with the series after a while—I'm not personally turned on by vampires and werewolves—so it's possible that I missed some of the changes in Anita that Fruend and Guyant addressed. Perhaps there is stronger evidence in the later books.

But I wish the panel had focused on some of the other work available in showing the truly transgressive nature of women warriors. An analysis of the various warriors in the Elemental Logic series by Laurie J. Marks[2] would provide substantial fodder for discussion. The Marks series upends a number of givens related both to gender and warriorship, and, in fact, provides a very different approach to fighting off an invasion.

The work of Nicola Griffith would also present a valuable perspective. The character of Aud Torvingen[3] provides excellent material for discussion of the woman warrior as just warrior. Aud does, I think, look for justice, but her willingness to go to extremes in pursuit of it can be shocking. Certainly, Aud is transgressive.

Interestingly, both Marks and Griffith provide examples of transgressive sexuality as well. In the world of the Elemental Logic series, same sex relationships are treated equally with male/female ones, and the family has been redefined much more broadly. Griffith's Aud is a lesbian very comfortable with her own sexuality. In both cases,

2 *Fire Logic*, 2002; *Earth Logic*, 2004; *Water Logic*, 2007.

3 *The Blue Place*, 1999; *Stay*, 2003; *Always*, 2007.

I find the sexuality much more of a challenge to conventional ideas than that presented in Hamilton's books.

A look at the work of Joanna Russ and Suzy McKee Charnas is important to any discussion of fictional women warriors. Russ's work, and a lot of Charnas's, was written in the 1970s and 1980s, but their stories set the standard. For that matter, Marion Zimmer Bradley's Renunciates in her Darkover series provide a fascinating look at the difficulties faced by women willing to fight in a particularly sexist world.

Other authors whose work about women warriors would be worth discussing include Elizabeth Lynn, Elizabeth Moon, Elizabeth Bear, and C.J. Cherryh. In different ways, all of them give us women warriors who push the boundaries of our current societal limitations on women. I find their work much more transgressive than that of Hamilton.

I hope Fruend and Guyant will continue to explore the transgressive woman warrior as presented in fiction and expand their focus to include some of the powerful work available on the subject.

Works Cited

Moore, Nancy Jane, "We Aren't Civilized Yet: Reflections from the WisCon 30 Panel on Women Warriors," In *The WisCon Chronicles, Vol. 1*, ed. L. Timmel Duchamp, 132-142. Seattle: Aqueduct Press, 2007.

Marks, Laurie J., *Fire Logic*. New York: Tor, 2002.

———. *Earth Logic*. New York: Tor, 2004.

———. *Water Logic*. Small Beer Press, 2007.

Griffith, Nicola, *The Blue Place*. New York: Harper, 1999.

———. *Stay*. New York: Vintage, 2003.

———. *Always*. New York: Riverhead, 2007.

Excerpt from "Ghosts of New York"

Jennifer Pelland

Poets and sages like to say that there is clarity in certain death. That a calm resignation settles over the nearly deceased, and they embrace the inevitability of the end of life with dignity and grace.

But there was no clarity for her, no calmness, no life flashing before her eyes in a montage of joys and regrets. There was just pure animal terror, screams torn from her throat as she plummeted towards the ground in the longest ten seconds of her life.

And then there was an explosion of pain.

She remembered flailing at the air, as if she could somehow sink her nails into it and cling there until help arrived. She remembered the crash and pop of the people who were landing mere seconds before her. She remembered a fleeting moment of shame when her dress blew up over her head, exposing her underwear to the crowds gathered below. She remembered the burst of shit and piss as she crashed through the awning just a split second before she hit—

The only people who find clarity in certain death are those who somehow cheat it, those who can reflect back upon the experience and use it to goad them into living a better life.

For the ghosts, there is only terror.

After her first fall, she stood by the roadkill smear that was her body, not recognizing what she was seeing at first, until two more bodies rained down from above, splattering on pavement with a crash of glass and a sickening splat.

Then she knew.

Then the North Tower collapsed.

All around her, people screamed and ran while she stood helplessly by the wreckage of her body. Debris flew through her, burying her corpse, leaving the ghost of her untouched.

And then she fell again.

If anything, it was worse than the first time. Now, it was an echo of a fall, a non-existent body falling from a non-existent building, with all the terror of the original fall—the same flailing, the same flash of embarrassment, the same piss—

The same body-shattering moment of pain at the end.

Days passed, the dust cleared, the debris and bodies were carried away, but still she fell, over and over, sinking through the sky for the same interminably long ten seconds, the pain of impact fresh and raw each and every time.

Between falls, she wondered if she were in hell. She wondered what terrible thing she'd done in life to merit this kind of eternal punishment. But she couldn't remember.

She couldn't remember anything.

No, that wasn't strictly true. In the chest-heaving intervals between falls, she could remember, if she tried, the blistering heat and choking smoke. She remembered mobbing a broken window with a half-dozen other people, gulping in precious lungfuls of clean air. She remembered a floor too hot to stand on, the eerie creak of metal. She remembered a man and a woman dropping past her window, hand in hand. She remembered looking over her shoulder at the impenetrable wall of smoke. She remembered a scream stuck in her throat, a heart that felt like it would burst through her chest, a desperate wish to breathe just once more before she died.

She remembered a split-second decision, legs suddenly unfrozen, propelling her out into the blue September sky.

But before that?

Nothing.

[End excerpt]

It took me seven years to be able to write about 9/11. I remember reading Tom Junod's excellent article "The Falling Man" on *Esquire Magazine*'s website when it first came out, but was still too close to the events to transform my horror into art. For those who haven't read the article, it's about Junod's search for the identity of the subject of Richard Drew's infamous photo of one of the jumpers. I re-read the article in 2008, and couldn't stop thinking about just how many people had jumped, and what they must have gone through for that to be the only logical decision to make, and why we needed to pretend that they hadn't existed. And that thought became a story.

No short story I've written has made me this nervous. I have no personal connection to 9/11—no one I know died that day, and I live outside Boston, not in NYC or DC, so my city wasn't physically scarred by that day (although I believe Boston bore a burden of unwarranted guilt over two of the planes having taken off from our airport). To make sure I hadn't written anything inadvertently offensive, I ran it past a couple of friends of mine with strong NYC ties, and they gave it enthusiastic thumbs up. Still, it was a story that I put into circulation with trepidation, and by WisCon 2009, I still hadn't sold it.

I read the story aloud for the first time that WisCon, and before I started, I warned people what it was about and told them I wouldn't be offended if they had to leave. I understood it could easily be a trigger for people who'd lost loved ones on that day. Three people walked out, everyone else stayed until the end. I wasn't bothered by the walkouts—in fact, my heart ached for them. For me, 9/11 was a national tragedy. For them, it was a personal one. The last thing I want to do with my fiction is use it to hurt people who are already hurting. So for once, I'm grateful for my walkouts, which is something I never thought I'd say.

* "Ghosts of New York" was published in Apex Book's *Dark Faith* anthology in May 2010.

Jennifer Pelland lives outside of Boston with an Andy, three cats, and an impractical amount of books. Several of her short stories have been collected in her book *Unwelcome Bodies* from Apex Books, who will also be publishing "Ghosts of New York" in their *Dark Faith* anthology. For more: http://www.jenniferpelland.com.

Carl Brandon Society meeting at WisCon 33.
Left to right: Nisi Shawl, Diantha Sprouse, Victor J. Raymond, Candra K. Gill, MJ Hardman, Claire Light
(photo by D Bautista)

Isabel Schechter and Johanna at the POC dinner
(photographer unknown)

Beverly Friend, dressed in style
(photo by I Kaplan)

Sylvia Kelso and Anne Sheldon
at the CBS/Aqueduct Party
(photo by D Bautista)

Nisi Shawl and June Cotton in the Dealers' Room
(photo by S Kelso)

Nancy Jane Moore at the Aqueduct reading (photo by K Wilham)

Diantha Sprouse shows off her self-created crown at the at the CBS/Aqueduct party (photo by D Bautista)

Andrea Hairston at the Aqueduct reading (photo by K Wilham)

MJ Hardman at the CBS/Aqueduct party with Nisi and Nancy Jane in the background (photo by D Bautista)

Victor J Raymond models his dragonfly crown while signing up new CBS members at the party (photo by D Bautista)

Camille Alexa reading at Michelangelo's coffee shop (photo by K Green)

Dimas Bautista at the CBS/Aqueduct party with guest Margie Peterson (photo by MJ Hardman)

Eleanor Arnason at the Aqueduct reading (photo by K Wilham)

Erin Ranft and Lawrence Schwegler presenting their papers (photo by ML Gardin)

Venturestein Unbound: Male Generative Power in *Frankenstein* and *The Venture Brothers*

Zach Wellhouse

One powerful interpretation of the Frankenstein myth that has waned in popularity in the face of such contemporary touchstones as General Mills' Frankenberry cereal and the bolt-necked neon green Halloween monster is how it dramatically lays bare the masculine desire to create life. In "Possessing Nature: The Female in *Frankenstein*," Anne K. Mellor explains Victor Frankenstein's maniac urge to build a monster as "stealing the female's control over reproduction" (1996, 274). By this interpretation his hubris is not just pushing the boundaries of science beyond their healthy levels—into the realm of God—but his intrusion into the feminine domain, seizing the power of his contemporaries for himself. Mellor reacts negatively to Frankenstein's seizure, claiming that he has "eliminated the female's primary biological function and source of cultural power" (274). Newer works that refer back to the commonly accepted images of the Frankenstein myth, without the feminist ramifications, serve to dilute the original connotations until all that's left are scenes of muscle-bound violence and mobs armed with pitchforks and torches. Without exposure to the original text, casual consumers of *Frankenstein*-related merchandise would be unaware of the feminist currents attached to the property. Cartoon Network's *The Venture Brothers* subverts this trend. Although not a show about *Frankenstein* on the surface, the references to Mary Shelley's text and theories of gender provide a solid point for contemporary discussion of the conflation of scientific advancement and masculine creative urges.

The Venture Brothers chronicles the adventures of failed super-scientist Dr. Thaddeus "Rusty" Venture while raising two cloned sons. The show's tone constantly wavers between parody of action cartoons and more heartfelt attempts to complicate the genre. The parodic elements are in the forefront when Venture's arch-nemesis is revealed to be a shrill-voiced man in a monarch butterfly costume who belongs to a ruthlessly bureaucratic crime organization known as the Guild of Calamitous Intent. Comedy is less evident in sequences such as when Venture's bodyguard, Brock Sampson, searches for spiritual guidance after being asked to procure human corpses to fuel Venture's proposed "Venturestein" project. I contend that episodes such as the latter, as well as the show's general concern with clone issues, catapult *The Venture Brothers* into conversations surrounding Mary Shelley's *Frankenstein*, offering reinforcement of the feminist themes found in the novel with a deal of eloquence that is exceptional for the show's time slot and target audience.

Contemporary critics across message boards and non-academic review sites tend to agree with Amazon.com reviewer Paul Gaita in praising *The Venture Brothers'* "[e]xceptionally sharp writing that's rich with pop culture references" (2007). However, reviews of this sort often miss the intertexual action responding to areas outside of the domain typically claimed by popular culture—including *Star Wars* and obscure rock bands from the 1980s. By viewing the show in this reductive light, it is merely a combination of postmodern parody and homage to masculine action programs such as *Johnny Quest* and *G.I. Joe.* Other critics, such as Popmatters.com's Michael Abernathy, do not give the show even that much credit, explaining, "my nightmares are more enjoyable than this infantile series" (2004). However, it can be argued that the show's system of cultural references does more. *The Venture Brothers* reverses the trend of uncritical *Frankenstein* knock-offs, such as the 1988 made-for-television movie *Scooby Doo and the Ghoul School,* which deals only in empty images, capitalizing on a familiar, blocky, blue-green face. Instead, *The Venture Brothers* triumphs by engaging with the original work's theme of unfulfilled masculine creative urges, especially as they encroach on the feminine domain. In his endless scientific experiments—especially the cloning of human beings—Dr. Venture demonstrates his subconscious desire to gain command over feminine power and bring balance to his neurotic life. Through its references of the Frankenstein myth as well as other cultural properties deriving from Mary Shelley's novel, *The Venture Brothers* reveals sympathies at odds with the irreverent nature of its jokes: the importance of a stable, nuclear family and mistrust of unchecked scientific growth. This intertextual response enhances the layers of meaning in the program while defending the legacy of the original work from other contemporary products.

The crux of the connection between *Frankenstein* and *The Venture Brothers* is human cloning. Although Frankenstein's monster is a reanimated corpse rather than a series of genetically identical copies, the moral concerns are similar enough that literary and popular sources have made comparisons between the two techniques. Iina Hellsten specifically examines the construction of clone metaphors in "Dolly: Scientific Breakthrough or Frankenstein's Monster? Journalistic and Scientific Metaphors of Cloning." Despite not being a reanimated corpse, Dolly the cloned sheep was popularly compared to Frankenstein's monster in news articles because they were both formed through "unnatural" processes.

Frankenstein's monster has become a metaphor with many assumptions behind it, spoken and unspoken (Hellsten 2000, 214). Not only is the public mind's conception of cloning here modified by allusions to Frankenstein, but *Frankenstein* itself serves as a starting point for exploring contemporary concerns regarding scientific creation of life. This comparison mirrors how Frankenstein images are mass-produced today; the positive aspects are present in the identical copies of texts that allow for democratized discourse across great distances and with little cost. The negative implications of the term suggest discount toy stores seeking to unload pallets of unsold action figures of Frankenstein's monster from 2004's critically unhelpful (and universally panned) *Van Helsing*. The reference to Venture's cloning facility as a "Dracula/Frankenstein factory" by a character unversed in scientific minutiae demonstrates the linguistic danger of sliding definitions in contemporary discussions ("Viva los Muertos," 2006).

Although male creation stories have older roots than *Frankenstein,* the novel remains integral to cloning discussions because it is the first canonical work to explicitly posit the moral complexities of non-divine forms of creation. When the power enters the hands of a fallible man rather than the divine Christian God or unknowable Zeus, it takes on an additional dimension of relevancy. Janeen Webb agrees: "the Frankenstein metaphor remains appropriate in any discussion of clones in science fiction, simply because the nature/nurture problem is at the very root" (2002, 158). Did the creature destroy everything that it touched because Victor refused to teach it, instead decrying it as "a thing such as even Dante could not have conceived" or because it was part of his essential nature (Shelley 1996, 35)? Similarly, are human clones destined to cheapen the experience of human life, or is proper tutelage all that is necessary? We see this dilemma visualized in *The Venture Brothers* with every innocent blunder made by Venture's sons, Hank and Dean. Venture exasperatedly explains, "Look, if you have a clumsy child, you make them wear a helmet. If you have death-prone children, you keep a few clones of them in your lab" ("Powerless in the Face of Death," 2006).

With the Frankenstein/cloning connection discussed, I would like to turn to the rotten personal lives of the key scientists, and why it's so dangerous. In "The Zeus Syndrome: Womb Envy and Male Pregnancy," Maria Ferreira utilizes mythic and psychoanalytic theory to explore the masculine desire to create life. Her guiding concept is Karen Horney's concept of womb envy, first put forward in 1932's "The Dread of Woman." This theory is a reversal of the Freudian penis envy: man desires the female capacity to create life, and sublimates the urge in various ways. Frequently this is through literary or scientific discourse, as both are forms of creation. Within the literary realm, treatments of alchemy and more modern speculative sciences such as genetic engineering provide less masked visions of desire. Through clone sciences, man is able to create what his biology has denied him. Ferreira approves of these instances in her case studies, commenting on how the androgyny of the male mother serves to weaken culture-based formations of gender as dependent on sex.

Ferreira's emphasis on culture-based gender traits is integral to my thesis. I am not simply proposing that Frankenstein and Venture (and in turn, their creations) are flawed because they lack upbringing in traits that are "innately feminine." Instead, it is that they lack the traits that Western society has traditionally assigned to feminine caregivers, and their masculine educations were unable to compensate.

Rusty Venture's womb envy has a different source than Horney proposes, but the end result is the same. His driving goal is to be worthy of his heroic father's name by continuing the dead Jonas Venture's super-science legacy—especially his cloning projects.

Clone research stands as the one area where the younger Venture arguably surpasses his father: the mad Mr. Brisby says as much after kidnapping Rusty in hopes of living forever ("The Incredible Mr. Brisby," 2004). By focusing his generative energy on his personal projects, Rusty is able to ignore his abysmal, conventional interactions with women and explore an alternate form of completeness. When he meets his childhood friend, Dr. Tara Quymm, in the depths of the jungle, they try to resume their youthful romance. Here, Rusty reveals that he has not had sex in "nineteen years, two months, and four days" ("Dr. Quymm, Medicine Woman," 2008). His desire to live up to his father's standards have intertwined with his desire to create, to leave his mark on the world, driving his life and ruining his works, professional and private.

Victor Frankenstein shows a similar inability to interact with women. Despite his proclamation, "I love Elizabeth, and look forward to our union with delight," he proves it only after a two-year vacation in England (Shelley, 132). Were he truly convinced of their compatibility he would pay more attention to her own needs when musing, "Elizabeth approved of the reasons of my departure, and only regretted that she had not the same opportunities of enlarging her experience and cultivating her understanding" (106). According to Ferreira's presentation of male generative substitutes, Frankenstein's passionless marriage prospects are not because of latent homosexuality (as suggested by Mellor and others), but repressed womb envy and its expression, scientific narcissism: "the drive to doubling and duplication, to producing replicas of themselves...a form of protection against extinction" (Ferreira 2005, 129). Rusty Venture does the same thing with his self-titled Venturestein project (and also with his sons); not only is Venturestein new life that shares the doctor's name, but its profitability will insure that his reputation lives on even after he is dead.

In the episode "Viva los Muertos!" Rusty creates a monster similar to Frankenstein's, naming it after himself. Although Venturestein is quick to call Rusty "father," the super-scientist quashes that notion: "I get enough of that from these two," he comments, referring to his nearby sons, Hank and Dean. Like Venturestein, Venture's sons are artificial creations; unlike Venturestein, they originally had a mother. The Venture mother's absence in the show is notable, emphasizing how the lack of balance between masculine and feminine sources has far-reaching consequences. Dr. Byron Orpheus, the Ventures' tenant, became a single father after his wife left him; The Monarch, Venture's deranged arch-nemesis, lost both of his parents only to be raised by a herd of monarch butterflies; Venture himself never had a mother's guiding hand. It would be reductive to say that everyone on the show directly suffers from a lack of mother figures, but it is worth mentioning that characters with happy family lives are few and far between.

In the exchange where Venture rejects the fatherly duty of caring for his creation, the viewer is reminded of Frankenstein's similar dismissal: "I beheld the wretch—the miserable monster whom I had created" (Shelley, 35). Despite such repudiations, Frankenstein's creation recognizes the patriarchal rights and responsibilities of his progenitor. He turns to Frankenstein to build him a mate, begging, "Oh! my creator, make me happy, let me feel gratitude towards you for one benefit!" (99). Despite his great strength, the monster positions himself in the inferior position of a child asking a father to use his superior worldly powers to demonstrate his love. Venturestein's pathetic attempts to enter the Venture family are much the same.

Once Venture and Frankenstein recognize the responsibility of tending their creations, they both become more ambivalent toward them. They are both concerned with the power granted by the act of creation, unprepared for the compassion for which both monsters plead. This deficiency can be traced to the limited female contact that shaped both men while growing up.

Although it could be argued that Frankenstein had ready access to the influence of his mother and Elizabeth, he was distanced from them through social factors. Despite his high praise of Elizabeth, Frankenstein concludes his initial description of her by saying, "I loved to tend on her, as I should on a favourite animal" (Shelley, 20). Despite her many admirable talents, she remains in the separate, discrete realm of animals and whimsy common to a woman of her era. Frankenstein's mother, as will be explored below, lacked the authority to properly influence her son. Because neither male scientist had early exposure to the value of society-determined feminine traits, their masculine sides were allowed to expand without limit. Femininity represented uncertain mystery—as indicated by

Venture and Frankenstein's awkwardness with women—opposed to the black-and-white violence of Jonas Venture's world and the unchecked scholasticism encouraged by Frankenstein's father. The content of the schooling isn't important to Alphonse Frankenstein, who "thought it necessary, for the completion of [Victor's] education, that [he] should be made acquainted with other customs" (24). Through this push and the electrical experiments from Victor's youth, Alphonse demonstrates only the acquisition of knowledge, failing to provide any purpose or restraint. The only way to understand the traditional female domains of empathy and restraint was to possess their most visible and mysterious process: the creation of life.

Whatever Frankenstein's mother taught him about human interaction never had fertile ground in which to grow. The egalitarian nature in which she treated him failed to provide the moral guidance that Shelley suggests would have halted his obsessive mania. Reflecting on his childhood he recalls, "my mother partook of our enjoyment. Neither of us possessed the slightest pre-eminence over the other; the voice of command was never heard amongst us" (24). Since Frankenstein's mother does not seem to have assumed a position of authority with her child, his alchemy-and-science view of the world leaves him malformed. All he knows of being female are fun and a specific sort of kindness, lacking in authority. Neither lesson is of use to him in the science-minded halls of the University of Ingolstadt where his view of limitless progress is allowed to further grow.

M. Waldman, one of Frankenstein's two guides in academic manhood, furthers the split between science and the feminine domain while highlighting the generative aspect of science. Waldman gives Frankenstein a list of orders regarding how to act if "his wish is to become really a man of science, and not merely a petty experimentalist" (28). Here, the man of science is a hyper-masculine extension of Frankenstein's early studies in alchemy—one who can create new forms instead of merely observing and theorizing. Without any outside morals to complicate the situation, Frankenstein seizes upon the image of the man of science and takes it to its furthest extent.

Rusty Venture's mother is never conclusively introduced, nor does he have any other female role models in his youth. Venture's most salient exposure to women in his youth is depicted in a flashback in which he recalls playing jungle explorer with the young

Dr. Quymm during one of his father's swinger parties. Venture's first, innocent kiss is interrupted by the drunken flailing of his father, who is too distracted by his paramour to notice the location of his son's blanket fort ("Dr. Quymm, Medicine Woman"). This one-sided view of women as objects for fun sex is exacerbated by Venture's jet-setting, hyper-masculine childhood. His entire youth is spent as a "boy adventurer," assisting his father on globe-spanning explorations of lost civilizations and demonstrations of 1950s scientific optimism. It is likely that his fate is sealed by the time that he is five years old when he is forced to kill a man with a house key to earn his father's approval ("The Family That Slays Together, Stays Together, Part II," 2008). He is entirely split from the shared world of men and women, existing solely in the domain of unrealistic, male-focused adventure fiction.

Apparently lacking in traditionally valued female socialization, Dr. Venture and Frankenstein seek to synthesize it later in their lives. Women have become the Other—the unknowable, that which is different. They symbolically confront one of the exclusive traits of this Otherness—the creation of life—through the creation of extra-human monsters. This connection is one that contemporary fan-critics such as Todd Alcott consciously notice. In his review of "Viva los Muertos," Alcott explains, "parenting isn't always just a nurturing instinct born of love, it can also spring from a desire to mold and warp, to control and shape an unformed mind" (2006). Frankenstein recoils from the kind of hands-on control that Dr. Venture provides his creation, but nevertheless seeks to control the major decisions in its life, including its happiness and ability to have a mate.

Fearing the material results of the prevalence of male cloning fantasies, Robyn Morris paints the issue as one of ideological control She argues that mainstream literature—and the majority of science fiction works—present a world "in which humanness is constructed as white, male, Western, and heterosexual, but also [where] whiteness constructs and continually reconstructs itself as naturally *not other* within mainstream texts such as...*Frankenstein*" (2004, 93). Essentially, it's the "unmarked state" that I learned about during the WisCon 33 cultural appropriation panel. In this case the hegemonic male becomes the default human being who seeks to extend his power through duplication and re-defining that which is different as monstrous. Within this system, clones are the ultimate binary-breakers. Since they are cast out from polite, hegemonic society, their identities are fluid sites that agitate the status quo. Neither man nor beast, living nor dead, they are hybrid creations that challenge stable worldviews. The gut response that clones and laboratory monsters are unnatural subversions of life, or the theft of divine generative powers, is hegemonic society's way of expressing displeasure at the questions of self raised by artificial life. What is life if it can no longer be explained as "not dead"? Hegemonic, hyper-masculine control is able to marginalize clones, but never quite domesticate them. Venturestein breaks free from his shackles where he is forced to absorb subliminal military tutorials, just as Frankenstein's creature pursues his creator for closure regarding his existential purpose. Framed as not quite human, clones (and to continue the extended metaphor, non-hegemonic figures including women) are recast as monsters to be pitied or feared, but never treated equally. As a result the personal problems of Venture and Frankenstein become issues of relevance to society as a whole.

Even more shocking examples of hybridity are Hank and Dean Venture, Rusty's "sons." They are especially troubling within Morris's scheme because they mirror the exterior appearance of natural humans. Indeed, it is not revealed that they are clones until the end of *The Venture Brothers*' first season. The Venture brothers have each died fourteen times, only to have their memories uploaded into new bodies. Upon finally confronting their own hybrid Other nature by discovering their birth-laboratory, the boys react with shock and fall into what Brock describes as, "some sort of saw-their-own-clones" coma. Only Rusty's quick lies that the clones were meant as Christmas presents, "ready to think you're the coolest and do your chores" are enough to re-impose the hegemonic slave state on the boys and return them to their subjugated worldview ("Viva los Muertes"). Although the backup clones in the laboratory are presented as servants, it is Hank and Dean who end up helping their father with his money-making schemes; the boys are only valued for acting in their prescribed roles as underlings and good sons.

Although Hank and Dean know about their backup clones by the end of the second season, they believe themselves to be the originals. Over the third season of the show, this becomes increasingly unlikely as Dean pieces together the totality of their marginalized state. The realization that they are caught between the elaborate "game" of their father's super-science adventurism and everyday life begins to crystallize. Existing as pawns has reduced them to second-class citizens in the eyes of their father (who mistakes heat stroke for "lollygagger's syndrome") and left them unable to live conventional lives due to the antiquated subliminal learning tapes that they listen to in lieu of schooling ("ORB," 2008). One reason that their father doesn't care for them is because he can always clone a new batch; their deaths have become a laughing matter. During one montage of all of the deaths that the boys go through, Brock and Rusty break out in uncontrolled laughter, remembering the ridiculous facial hair that they had in their younger years. ("Powerless in the Face of Death.") Each boy reacts to the vast gulf between their lives and "normalcy" in a different way: Hank cheers as all of the backup clones are destroyed in a gory battle sequence, adopting his father's callousness toward his army of brothers. Dean suffers panic attacks, underscoring his oppression with the forced helplessness of heart trouble, dizziness, and shortness of breath ("The Family That Slays Together, Stays Together, Part II"). Although unable to articulate the problem, his body is aware of the wrongness of its situation.

Consider the similarities between the Venture brothers' marginalized state and that of Frankenstein's monster, who gains his education through white, hegemonic books and observing civilization through a crack in the wall. Despite his physical proximity to this ideal family, he is irreconcilably distanced from it. He is aware of what he is not, and cannot be, but society offers no mechanism for him to belong. In taking control of female creative force, Frankenstein has cut himself off from understanding female power on its own terms, and the price he pays is wreaked upon society, his family, and his child—the monster. None are happy with the result.

This leaves us with the concluding question: who is the real monster here? Hegemonic, masculine society argues that it is everything which is unable to meet the requirements of its binary, standardizing categories: the Other. That's not very helpful. Feminist critics of Shelley and the creators of *The Venture Brothers* suggest that the villain is sublimated male fear of feminine power. Without a strong female influence to counter masculine cultural forces, the female domain becomes one to be feared and controlled. Given the usual construction of the Frankenstein myth, it's worthy of critical attention that *The Venture Brothers* engages more powerfully with Shelley's *Frankenstein* than many other contemporary sources. In the process, the show invites its users to confront serious issues of gender, gender roles, and marginalized subjects within a fun, non-threatening environment.

Works Cited

Abernathy, Michael. "The Venture Brothers | PopMatters Television Review." *Pop Matters.* 24 August 2004. November 2008. http://www.popmatters.com/tv/reviews/v/venture-brothers.shtml.

Alcott, Todd. "Venture Bros: Viva los Muertos!" Weblog Entry. *What Does The Protagonist Want?* 01 October 2006. 23 October 2008. http://toddalcott.livejournal.com/48273.html.

"Dr. Quymm, Medicine Woman" *The Venture Brothers* (Season 3). Perfs. James Urbaniak, Chris McCulloch, Patrick Warburton. Cartoon Network, 2008.

Ferreira, Maria. "The Zeus Syndrome: Womb Envy and Male Pregnancy." In *I Am the Other: Literary Negotiations of Human Cloning*, 109-144. Westport, CN: Praeger, 2005.

Gaita, Paul. "Amazon.com: The Venture Brothers: Season 2." Amazon.17 April 2007. November 2008. http://www.amazon.com/Venture-Bros-Season-Two/dp/B000M7XRC4.

Hellsten, Iina. "Dolly: Scientific Breakthrough or Frankenstein's Monster? Journalistic and Scientific Metaphors of Cloning." *Metaphor and Symbol* 15.4 (2000): 213.

Mellor, Anne K. "Possessing Nature: The Female in *Frankenstein*." In *Frankenstein*, ed. J. Paul Hunter, 274-286. New York: W.W. Norton and Company, 1996.

Morris, Robyn. "'What Does it Mean to be Human?': Racing Monsters, Clones and Replicants." *Foundation* 33.91 (2004): 81.

"ORB" *The Venture Brothers* (Season 3). Perfs. James Urbaniak, Chris McCulloch, Patrick Warburton. Cartoon Network, 2008.

"Powerless in the Face of Death" *The Venture Brothers* (Season 2). Perfs. James Urbaniak, Chris McCulloch, Patrick Warburton. DVD. Cartoon Network, 2006.

Shelley, Mary. *Frankenstein*. Ed. J. Paul Hunter. Norton Critical Edition. New York: Norton, 1996.

"The Family That Slays Together, Stays Together, Part II" *The Venture Brothers* (Season 3). Perfs. James Urbaniak, Chris McCulloch, Patrick Warburton. Cartoon Network, 2008.

"The Incredible Mr. Brisby" (Season 1). Perfs. James Urbaniak, Chris McCulloch, Patrick Warburton. DVD. Cartoon Network, 2004.

"¡Viva los Muertos!" *The Venture Brothers* (Season 2). Perfs. James Urbaniak, Chris McCulloch, Patrick Warburton. DVD. Cartoon Network, 2006.

Webb, Janeen. "Bone of My Bones, Flesh of My Flesh: A Brief History of the Clone in Science Fiction." In Biotechnological and Medical Themes in Science Fiction, ed. Domna Pastourmatzi, 152-164. Thessaloniki, Greece: University Studio Press, 2002.

Zach Welhouse is currently working toward his MA in English with an emphasis on cultural studies at Kansas State University. This was his first year at WisCon, but it won't be the last.

Famous Monsters of Filmland

Gwynne Garfinkle

Christopher Lee pulls a stake
from his own chest in *Dracula*
Has Risen From the Grave.
Apparently vampires got harder
to kill in late sixties England.

They used to cut the scene
from *Frankenstein* where Karloff
hurls that girl in the water, thinking
her a flower. Monsters don't
always know they're doing wrong.

"This is not the sister you knew,
this is only a shell." Dracula knows.
He turns nice girls, daughters,
wives into peignoir-clad monsters,
a state devoutly to be wished.

Gwynne Garfinkle lives in Los Angeles. Her fiction and poetry have appeared in such publications as *Strange Horizons*, *Goblin Fruit*, *Space and Time*, and *Aberrant Dreams*. She's currently writing a novel that is a political ghost story set in 1970s New York.

Attending WisCon

My WisCon #4

Philip A. Weiss

I haven't even left Madison. I had intended to wait a few days after returning to Seattle to write about my WisCon experience. I'm sitting in Michelangelo's coffee shop, where I planned to read some of the books I bought. I sat down, pulled *Feeling Very Strange* from my backpack, and then just looked at it. My head is full of thoughts about my experience, and I don't think I can read. So I write instead, though this won't get published until I get home.

Why WisCon?

I decided to attend WisCon after the kerfuffle last year over what I wrote about Joe Abercrombie's *Before They Are Hanged*. Some commenters on Abercrombie's blog accused me of...well, I'll just quote one:

> Mr. Rat sounds like he's been brainwashed by the feminist lit department at his university, who read oppression into every interaction between men and women.

I thought this was quite amusing. I'd never taken a feminist lit class. Ever. I'd taken only the "Intro to the Canon" type of literature classes, and I don't mean the feminist canon. I attended the University of Idaho. Idaho! In the center of the whitest Congressional district in the USA at the time. A state where the women's groups that get any attention are headed by Phyllis Schlafly. This was after attending a high school run by the Catholic church and only a decade away from being an all-boys prep school. Don't even get me started on my elementary and junior high education! There I was taught that dinosaur fossils were planted by the devil's minions to trick us.

The point being, no one has ever indoctrinated me in proper or even improper feminist theory.

But afterward, I thought perhaps I should learn more. I subscribed to FeministSF—The Blog!, Angry Black Woman, and others. My friend Kim planned on attending WisCon last year and told me about it, encouraging me to go. Last year I had Mom's illness and impending death to deal with, so I didn't. Kim attended and returned with awesome things to say about her experience. Earlier this year, I decided to go.

Introversion and Culture

I'm not the most extroverted of people. A fair number of people seem surprised that I am shy. I can fake outgoingness sometimes. The best comparison I have to the trepidation I felt about WisCon is my experience going to India. I was stepping into a foreign culture. India has values about which I was not familiar. The country has unwritten rules of which I was completely unaware. I went by myself, without a protective posse. I stood out as not being part of the locally dominant culture. All these things worked against me in India, and all of these elements were present to some degree with attending WisCon.

I did two things (at least) though to make things easier on myself. My first tactic I chose consciously. I would not open my mouth to express any opinion in any panel programming. Questions were fine. Requesting clarification I thought was safe. But I decided against expressing any sort of opinion.

I learned this from a mentor fifteen years ago. He told me, "Your job is just to listen right now."

It was a different context, but the issue was the same. I am an opinionated guy, and I have an instinctive reaction to spout my opinion to any and all who come within earshot (or read my crap online). Regardless if I was asked for my opinion. Regardless if I have any background information. Regardless if I knew the reasons why other people had their opinions. I'm better than I was nearly half a lifetime ago, but I'm still pretty bad about it.

That's the intellectual reason to keep my mouth shut. It's valid, but the driving force was emotional. I fear being wrong. I fear being attacked. I fear getting jumped on. My fear is not rational. Others may have a perfectly rational fear of attack. I do not. I have lived and learned from every personal attack. I've thrived even. Yet every time I write something negative about a book or express an opinion online, the pit of my stomach drops before I press publish.

I didn't consciously try to avoid controversy with my second choice, but I'm sure I subconsciously wanted just that. I picked panels to attend that were about interacting directly with books. I avoided second level discussions. For instance, I didn't attend a panel on online activism. I also picked topics with panelists whose names I knew.

For many, the most prominent issue this year was RaceFail. The people who were the most involved in RaceFail discussions on blogs were either names I didn't know well, or people who didn't come to WisCon. Writers of color (i.e., those with the most at stake immediately in RaceFail) that I've read and who were at WisCon included Nnedi Okorafor and...Nnedi Okorafor. And although RaceFail directly concerns literature, discussion about RaceFail is one level removed from books. Keeping my panels directly related to literature kept me one level away from RaceFail discussions. I did attend one panel on multiculturalism and thought it was great discussion, but I doubt it would register much controversy compared to other rooms.

I don't believe it was an accident that the things I consciously thought about when choosing panels led me away from scary stuff. If I go next year (and I'm leaning towards attending) I think I will examine the choices I've made to make sure I'm not avoiding difficult topics. Or at least, if I am avoiding them, it's a considered choice.

I'm not sure whether my panel choice strategy was a good thing or not. On one hand, I didn't freak myself out about a topic that won't be resolved for quite some time anyway. On the other hand, I learned about five percent of what I could have learned. Had I thought more, I might have chosen differently.

WisCon Programming

I'm not normally one to gush about anything, but the panels were chock full of substantive discussion. Sure, a few of them were fluff, and I enjoyed those of that ilk that I attended as well. In most time slots I circled at least two or three possible panels. Each panel had enough content to inspire at least one blog post from me. Some had enough for two or three.

WisCon 33 was not just my first WisCon, it was my first sf convention. Not being a con person, I don't know how much WisCon's panel selection/assignment method differs from other sf conventions. These panels have a mix of professionals and fans. Any attendees can put their names in the hat ahead of time to be on panels. I don't know how the programming committee selects folks, but it seemed to work out well for the most part. In only one case did it seem like a panelist was outclassed by the material and the rest of the panel.

In a couple of cases, the moderator could have done a better job leading the panel. Some kind of just were there, and their panels tended to ramble more. A couple panels had members who just had to talk. The moderator for one of those never showed. In the other case, the moderator himself was the person who dominated the discussion. None of them ruined their panels, but I would have liked to have heard more from some of the other panelists. Three moderators were outstanding: Fred Schepartz on the working class, L. Timmel Duchamp on book reviewing, and Jesse the K on feminist/leftist sf book groups.

The first panel I attended tackled the topic of the portrayal of the working class in speculative fiction, moderated by the aforementioned Fred Schepartz. I'm really no longer working class, but I still identify because I grew up in a working class family. My step-father was a union garbage man, and I'm no stranger to holding grunt positions either. I saw the panel topic and thought, "The sf books I read contain a lot of important people making important decisions, and it's really impersonal." The panelists talked about all the stereotypes of workers that get put into sf: lazy, stupid, and corrupt. They noted that sf lacking workers is often incomplete in its world building. Neglecting such things as who takes out the trash or who repairs the space station means that the world often only stands up to superficial scrutiny. Stuff just has to happen by magic. Thinking about who performs those tasks makes the writer think about how the details fit together.

The thoughts of the panelists mostly were that how workers are portrayed is a result of a couple of biases. First, that sf is often written with the big idea uppermost, in a top-down fashion, and the writer just never gets to the working classes. And second, that workers are not thought of as important, meaningful, or interesting.

I really enjoyed another panel on leftist sf book groups. A couple of years ago I attempted to start a book club on books conservatives considered harmful. It failed miserably despite some good initial interest. I wanted to know how I could do this successfully. Panelists came from Madison's "Beer and Marmalade" (B&M) and Chicago's "Think Galactic" (TG) reading groups. In starting up, TG papered the city with fliers, and the founders pressed their community of activists for possible members. B&M's initial members came from workers and customers at A Room of Ones Own. TG holds meetings at a bookstore, so both have a bookstore connection.

Besides those and other nuts and bolts items in the discussion, what really inspired me was the panelists' excitement with their groups. A lot of the discussions I heard during the convention came with an attitude of "it sucks that this is even an issue," where the talk in that panel felt like "OMG! I get to hang out with cool people and talk about stimulating topics!" This attitude simmers in the back of my mind still. The thought of starting such a group in Seattle occupies my brain.

Social Interaction

People come back to WisCon from all over the world year after year. It's not just a place for discussion of feminist topics. It's a place where people of like mind return for fellowship or sisterhood (to use both gender-loaded terms). It's an environment that can strengthen people's resolve before returning home to fight battles alone or in smaller groups.

There's a drawback to that, though. For the non-outgoing, there isn't a lot of support for integrating into the community, particularly in the first day or so, at least as far as I could tell.

Returning attendees eagerly embrace their friends from previous years, rejoicing at the end of the interruption of their camaraderie. Groups of friends unload their belongings and decamp to food or other activities, leaving the less connected behind. I'm sure not everyone experiences this, but I know I did, and several people I talked to related similar experiences of their first time attending.

The Gathering kicked off the social events on Friday. Among other things, it had tables for palm and tarot readings, e-zines, a fundraising table with ARCs to give away, a clothing swap, and a singing performance. But mostly it seemed to be standing in line waiting to participate in each activity. I took the opportunity to chat with a few folks while queuing, but the event was not a great place to mingle. The tables were interesting, though.

Friday night I attended the First WisCon Dinner, which seemed to have no support other than a line in the program guide. Ostensibly an event where a few experienced hands would welcome first timers to acculturate us, instead 25 of us newbies stood around at the designated meeting point wondering what the plan was supposed to be. We eventually split into three groups because the word from the local newbies was that nearby restaurants wouldn't be able to handle large groups. I quite enjoyed the small group I dined with, and chatted with Amy Sundberg and her husband Yonatan Zunger, from my group, throughout the convention.

I didn't hide out in my hotel room. I purposefully planted myself in the hotel lobby during breaks and periodically introduced myself to people. None of those conversations lasted long nor did any of those folks return to converse with me a second time during the first couple of days. I wasn't dismissed, but I didn't feel any real engagement either.

Someone first initiated conversation with me on day three. M. Rickert engaged me in an exchange Sunday morning, sensing I was bewildered and not pulled into the thick of things, sharing her first WisCon experience from a few years ago. I don't know the causes, whether our interaction was the key or something else was working, but I subsequently hooked into conversation with people better. That day I had lunch with Liz Henry, my friend Sara Linde, and a couple of others. Liz turned out to be wonderfully open to conversation. At the guest of honor speeches that night, my table seemed oddly magnetized to Seattleites. I think all but one of us hailed from my hometown. I felt far more comfortable by that point.

Authors

One big reason to go to WisCon was to find more good literature that I didn't know about. I bought books, and I got to meet some authors.

Though probably working off bad assumptions, I didn't chat too much with author panelists. I know they are real people. Most have day jobs. But I still have them on somewhat of a pedestal, and I didn't want to turn into a fanboy in the hallways. And neither could my puny brain come up with reasons to chat with them or with other panelists. In retrospect, the panel topic would have been a great icebreaker for me to chat with any panelist. Though in most cases I couldn't have chatted coherently on the panel topics immediately afterward anyway, even just to ask questions.

SignOut on Monday is kind of the designated fan event. A fair number of the authors in attendance set up at tables so folks can get their books signed. I bought a dozen or so books by authors and editors who attended and got them signed at SignOut: Geoff Ryman, Ellen Klages, David Schwartz, M. Rickert, Nnedi Okorafor, John Joseph Adams, Carol Emshwiller, and Nisi Shawl. In most cases I chatted a bit with them as well. Other than Ellen Klages and Geoff Ryman, most didn't have lines of more than one or two so I got to chat with them without interruption. Of course, all were friendly. I knew this, but I still felt surprised. Cue Bart Simpson: I will not put authors on pedestals. I will not put authors on pedestals.

I made a point to pick up something by M. Rickert to thank her for chatting with me Sunday. That turned out to be *Feeling Very Strange*, an anthology of slipstream stories. I've never read much slipstream though. I chatted with David Schwartz and M. Rickert (sitting side by side) who talked with me about the genre. I tend not to like literature I don't understand. Slipstream is designed around cognitive dissonance; by definition it will be hard to understand. But I wanted to try it out because I hadn't done so before, and M. Rickert writes slipstream. I may get something out of it, but I'm pretty sure the pieces that don't work for me *really* aren't going to work for me.

At the Sunday night Tiptree Award ceremonies, Nisi Shawl received, instead of the traditional chocolate, a pie. I thought I recognized a kindred pie aficionado, so when I got her to sign *Filter House*, I asked her about the chocolate replacement thing. Turns out she gets migraines from chocolate and thinks pie is the best thing ever. So I mentioned my own predilection for pie and how I made friends since 2002 by hosting Pie Night, an open invite party that's all about pie. Her response: "Where? Can I come?" I knew she lived in Seattle, and kind of hoped she'd want to come. Fanboy me emerges, though I haven't yet read anything she's written. But she seemed like one of the nicest and most thoughtful people on any of the panels I attended, so I wanted to get to know her.

Geoff Ryman also impressed me. I've only really read his story "V.A.O." before. I'm fairly familiar with his Mundane Manifesto and the movement he's trying to start. I appreciate the stance, but I enjoy non-Mundane sf too much to stick to stories that fit that mold only, as he has advocated at times. I attended one panel he was on, and had him sign a book at SignOut. Despite having only the limited interaction, when he ran into me on the streets of Madison this morning, he stopped to chat with me. Nothing substantive, but I was nevertheless impressed. There are a lot of people at WisCon and not all of them can register on a person's consciousness.

Next Year?

I can't say I've found my tribe yet. I don't bond deeply, quickly enough to make that assertion. Nevertheless, I found kindred spirits and content that serves my intellectual craving. I felt fulfilled like I haven't in a long time. There's something about engaging in deep discussion about books that I enjoy. I read a lot. It's hard to find people who read as much or as widely as I do. WisCon is full of people who outclass me in that respect. Full of people who outclass me in a lot of respects. That's stimulating.

Next year WisCon's guests of honor will be Mary Anne Mohanraj and Nnedi Okorafor. Both are thoughtful, intelligent, and extremely positive people, from all indications available to me. Their selection makes me want to go next year.

Philip A. Weiss reads a lot of books and spews his thoughts on them as King Rat at his blog Rat's Reading (http://reading.kingrat.biz/). Nisi did come Pie Night in July 2009, and Phil now brags that she liked his pies.

The Pause that Refreshes

Beverly Friend

Ensa reached towards the small pile of sticks carefully arranged in the ceremonial stone bowl on her bedside table. She pointed a long, slender finger towards the wood, and then just as she might have touched the nearest piece, hesitated. It was too early, barely dawn. She should wait for the others to arrive on this important day. Her daughters would soon join her as would the elders of the tribe. That is, the elder women; men had no role here today, and it was wise not to spark their envy.

She had already waited months for this day—actually eighteen months—to finalize her "Clearing." Oh, the frustration of the first six months, so marked by disappointment. Six times she had been so excited, so sure. Six times she had hoped, watched, and then failed, realizing that the right time had not arrived and that she must watch and wait again. Only twelve pure months could assure her readiness. She had already waited over five decades, happily greeting the arrival of each grey hair as a harbinger of her bright future.

She would be free now, the cycle of pain and responsibility over. Each day would be totally hers, open to her interests, even whims, as her powers grew. Today she would initiate her mastery of fire. Then who knew what else she might be able to control, what magic might fill her. Her mother had excelled at conjuring spirits. Grandmother, who had lived many years, ultimately had conquered the art of invisibility.

She rose and walked over to the mirror covering the wall opposite the bed, dropped her sleeping shift, turning as she did so to examine her naked body. Perhaps a little plump, she thought, but not bad for a woman who had borne four children. The two boys had come first. Of course she had loved them, but she had also been filled with sadness, knowing their limitations. And then two daughters had been born. What would soon be hers would some day be theirs, when they reached the right age.

Oh, it's not that men hadn't tried—first by prayer, later with drugs, even surgeries: all useless. Just as they could never conceive or bear children, so they could never achieve mastery of the elements. "Biology is Destiny," she thought. How fortunate she was to live in this time. Only in the past 200 years had women come to know what power was theirs. What history had *seen* negatively had been discovered to be the most powerful moment of life, a turning point, a renaissance of ability.

She dressed slowly, donning her white robe. She had made the finely woven garment herself. Carefully, she tied a bright red ribbon on her wrist. Then with gathering excitement she paced the floor, wringing her pale hands, now ordinary, but so soon to engage in magic. Oh, where was everyone? Surely, it was time.

She heard a footstep outside. Then the first woman entered. It was Kino, her mentor. As custom demanded, she said nothing, merely approached Ensa, and placing her hands on each flushed cheek, kissed her ceremonially on the forehead. Others soon followed—the elders—Nin, Archo, and Vira. Each with grey hair unbound, wearing long robes. Theirs were black, the only colorful relief offered by the slim red ribbon tied around their right wrists. Each also approached and kissed her before Kino led her to the circle of cushions on the floor and signaled her to sit.

Now only two more were expected—her daughters.

Sona and Syna arrived together, wearing grey robes. Their wrists were bare. They approached their mother, kissed her forehead, and sat down directly behind her.

Kino stood up and walked to the bowl of sticks on the bedside table. Carefully, she lifted it and brought it to Ensa. Putting it down on the floor before her, she resumed her seat.

All faces turned towards Ensa as the women raised their right hands in unison and untied the red ribbons, which drifted to the floor.

Kino spoke. "What bound is unbound. What tied is untied. What was is no more." They looked solemnly at Ensa, and Kino nodded for her to begin.

Trembling, Ensa unbound her own wrist and watched the ribbon fall. She lifted it and placed it on the sticks. Then, she solemnly licked the index finger of her right hand and reached out to touch the wood. For a moment, nothing happened, and fear gripped Ensa's heart. No, it must happen. Today was the day. Then, aware of a tingling sensation moving from fingertip to hand to arm, she saw a spark glowing—just where her finger had ever so lightly brushed the nearest twig.

Now the wood ignited, springing into flame, the red matching the ribbon, which also caught fire. Yes—she had achieved success. She looked triumphantly into the flames. Remembering the past, she gloried in the present. She had finally reached—what was that term the ancients had used—oh, yes, "Menopause."

Beverly Friend, PhD, Emeritus Professor of English, Oakton Community College and reviewer for www.chicagocritic.com, is a Science Fiction teacher and critic, and a founding member of the Science Fiction Research Association. She authored the text "Science Fiction: The Classroom in Orbit," and "The Science Fiction Fan Cult" (Northwestern University Dissertation).

Witches and Wizards: Gender and Power in Portrayals of Magic
Panel Thoughts

Beverly Friend

It was the very witching hour of the night when we gathered in our WisCon-coven. There we sat, facing an audience thirsty for knowledge.

Could we inform them? Could we haunt their thoughts? Why had I been asked to join this panel?

I sat, clutching my references—a colorless if solid historical pamphlet on witches and witch hunts and a vivid children's fantasy tome on witches and wizards, complete with illustrations. Was this enough? Was I ready for this?

In preparation, I'd made a handout. That is what teachers (even retired teachers) do. Often, I tell my students that I get paid by the number of handouts I create (with extra for those in on colored paper).

What did I know about witches? About wizards? What can be condensed into one page on a grid? Then, months after WisCon, an email arrived—the handout has outlived the con, taken on a life of its own, is requested by Sylvia Kelso for the WisCon Chronicles.

Who says magic is dead?

The witching hour is now long gone—and unfortunately, my mind has blanked on my fellow panel members. Perhaps the memory was stored in the long black cape and pointed hat I lost at the conference—or I would be happy to thank them. On the other hand, I was so inspired by another panel—the one on aging—that I wrote the preceding short story:

COMPARISON/CONTRAST, by Beverly Friend (Incomplete)

WITCH	*WIZARD*
PRIMARILY WOMEN	**PRIMARILY MEN**
I. ATTIRE	***I. ATTIRE***
Black Robe, Black Pointed Hat	Robe and Hat Not Limited to Black
Robe: Often Shabby or Torn	Robe: Often Regal and Embroidered
Usually Old and Ugly (Wart on Nose, Stooped)	Usually Old and Imposing (Tall, Erect, Bearded)
Carries Broom	Carries Staff or Magical Wand
II. SKILLS	***II. SKILLS***
Casts Spells/ Magical Powers (Conjuring) Associations with Healing	Casts Spells/ Vast Magical Powers (Via Demons)
Can be Good (or if Evil—on a Small, Personal Scale)	Can Be Good (or if Evil—on a Huge, Global Scale)
Familiar—Often a Cat	Familiar—Varied Possibilities
Makes Potions: Often Love Potions	Makes Potions: Often Alchemy
Association with Earth	Association with Metals
Gains Skill with Age, but no Formal Recognition.	Possible Prestige Promotion: Archmage, High Wizard
III. REPUTATION	***III. REPUTATION***
Most Likely Negative	Negative or Positive
"You Are a Witch" (Insult)	"You Are a Wizard" (Complement)
IV EMPLOYMENT	***IV EMPLOYMENT***
Often Self Employed	Often Hired by Royalty/ Prestige
V. LEARNING	***V. LEARNING***
Birth and/or Apprenticeships	Birth/ Apprenticeship/ Wizard Schools.
May Get Power from Sex With Devil (Fear Of Female Sexuality)	
VI. REACTIONS TO	***VI. REACTIONS TO***
Fear	Fear and Respect
Burned at the Stake	
TERMS: WITCH HUNT	**NEVER WIZARD HUNT**

Male Answer Syndrome: WisCon Panel Notes

Stef Maruch

(http://firecat.dreamwidth.org)

> Panel Description: Although it's not absolute, there's a strong tendency among masculine people to always want to have the definitive answer for everything, even if they don't necessarily know. In panels and elsewhere in life, it can be hard for men to admit they don't know things. Why is this? How can men deal with the pressure (either internal or external) to always have the right answer? How do women and other non-masculine folks deal with Male Answer Syndrome? If you think the answers to all these questions are obvious, then you need to come to this panel!"
>
> Panelists: Suzanne Allés Blom, Moondancer Drake, John Helfers, John H. Kim (moderator), Stef Maruch

In my pre-panel post, I said: "I wanted to be on this panel because it's All Answer Syndrome All The Time at my house...and the XY person in the relationship is not the only person participating. So I have experience from multiple sides. I also have funny stories and techniques that you'll want to know about!"

The moderator started out the panel with a live example of MAS. (He had mentioned in email discussions beforehand that he would do this, but we hadn't really come up with a whole role-playing strategy.) He rambled on about being offended at the notion of MAS and then promulgated a theory that the real problem isn't MAS but Female Silent Syndrome. He managed to go on for about three minutes before the audience started muttering. Then someone said "Did you do that on purpose?" and he said yes.

In my introductory statement I said that MAS is not limited to men. In my family of origin my mother was the one who did MAS and my father didn't. In my primary relationship, both my male partner and I do MAS. I also do MAS to my girlfriends. One of my sweeties has learned to say "rhetorical!" when she asks a rhetorical question because otherwise I will answer it, even though I know it's rhetorical. Sometimes if she complains about something to me, she has to remind me that she doesn't want advice. Sometimes I remember to ask if she wants advice.

I think there are several different kinds of behavior that could be described as "Male Answer Syndrome":

1. The urge to respond to a complaint or a request for sympathy by offering advice, rather than emotional comfort.
2. Feeling compelled to answer a question, even if it's rhetorical or joking. (For example, once I was at a con and jokingly asked "What's a pun?" Four people gave me the definition of pun. These were people who knew my command of English vocabulary pretty well.)
3. Pontificating. This is well described in the following article: "Men Explain Things to Me" by Rebecca Solnit (http://www.alternet.org/reproductivejustice/82222/).

> He...said to me, "So? I hear you've written a couple of books."
>
> I replied, "Several, actually."
>
> He said, in the way you encourage your friend's seven-year-old to describe flute practice, "And what are they about?"
>
> ...I began to speak only of the most recent on that summer day in 2003, *River of Shadows: Eadweard Muybridge and the Technological Wild West*, my book on the annihilation of time and space and the industrialization of everyday life.
>
> He cut me off soon after I mentioned *Muybridge*. "And have you heard about the very important Muybridge book that came out this year?"

> So caught up was I in my assigned role as ingénue that I was perfectly willing to entertain the possibility that another book on the same subject had come out simultaneously and I'd somehow missed it. He was already telling me about the very important book—with that smug look I know so well in a man holding forth, eyes fixed on the fuzzy far horizon of his own authority.
>
> ...Mr. Very Important was going on smugly about this book I should have known when Sallie interrupted him to say, "That's her book." Or tried to interrupt him anyway.
>
> But he just continued on his way. She had to say, "That's her book" three or four times before he finally took it in. And then, as if in a nineteenth-century novel, he went ashen. That I was indeed the author of the very important book it turned out he hadn't read, just read about in the *New York Times Book Review* a few months earlier, so confused the neat categories into which his world was sorted that he was stunned speechless—for a moment, before he began holding forth again.

Out of those three things, I feel compelled to give advice and answer questions, but I don't think I pontificate (others might think differently).

Some topics discussed on this panel

Why the behavior can be problematic.

- Moondancer said she was raised to be self-sufficient, and so when she doesn't know how to do something and her baby-daddy does, she wants him to teach her, not do it himself, but he will tend to try to do it himself.
- The pontificating kind of MAS is also problematic because it perpetuates the existing societal tendency for men to have more conversational space in the public sphere than women have.

- In some cases MAS is problematic because the answer offered is vague and/or it shuts down continued conversation.

Whether the behavior is in fact gendered.

- A woman whose partner was a transman said that when he was going to a support group he was recommended to read a book that encouraged him to take on mentoring/care-providing roles. (As a way of becoming/seeming/expressing more masculinity?)
- The same behavior is sometimes different coming from a man vs. coming from a woman. A woman in the audience said that she often gives answers at work, but she's perceived as being motherly and nurturing when she does that, rather than know-it-all or pontificating.

Are there cultural differences in how people offer MAS and respond to MAS?

- "Geek culture" is sometimes described as one in which being corrected is seen as a positive social interaction, whereas in some other cultures it's seen as a power play.
- MAS was unique to "our" culture. (But I don't remember what was meant by "our"— US? Western?)

Is MAS conscious or unconscious?

- In some cases it feels like there is something compulsory or automatic about it.
- At one point a woman in the audience pointed out that John Helfers had practiced MAS on moondancerdrake (she had said she was intimidated by people with higher education, and he began offering advice about that once it was his turn to speak). He seemed unaware that he had done it. His wife was in the audience, and she said that it wasn't really MAS because he had done it out of a nurturing urge, a discomfort with someone else's discomfort. (I still think it is MAS. I think the advice-giving form of MAS is one of the ways that people express nurturing.)

How to solve the problem of MAS?

- If it's the problem of giving advice instead of emotional support, one way is to learn to ask "Do you want comfort or suggestions right now?"

Stef Maruch opines about feminism, speculative fiction, fat activism, and more at http://firecat.dreamwidth.org. She lives in the San Francisco Bay Area and hates flying, but WisCon is worth it.

Panel Write-up: "Something Is Wrong on the Internet!"

Panel Description: "Something is wrong on the internet!" What keeps you going at 4 AM when there's so much fail, and only you and your fellow Internet drama addicts stand against it like stubborn superheroes? Let's talk about why Internet drama is important to us as activists and as fans, why we engage or disengage, and what it all means when ideas and personalities clash in public discussion of SF/F books, tv, fic, and culture.

Participants: Vito Excalibur (Moderator) Charlotte, Liz Henry, Piglet, Julia Starkey. *(Based on Liz Henry's liveblog of the panel, which was also edited by Julia Starkey.)*

Vito: SOMETHING IS WRONG ON THE INTERNET!

Piglet: When I'm bored I go online and see who's said something stupid, so I can flame out and get mad. Yay!

Vito: Something is often wrong on the internet. Wait, Liz are you liveblogging this?

Liz: Well...yes...I was kinda thinking...

Vito: Let's start off with the obvious: "It's just the internet, right? Why do you care?"

Julia: Why do I have to harsh people's squee? It's cool to just watch women of color be raped and murdered and colonized. Why can't I just chill out?

Vito: Yeah and why aren't you out there shooting someone in the head?

Julia: I go into a rage coma when people say that. A few years ago, at a WorldCon, there was a huge flame war in a panel about modernism in science fiction. If we can flame out over something H.G. Wells and Henry James wrote to each other in private correspondence, then we can damn well have a heated discussion over something as gross and disgusting as racism.

Vito: Does Internet drama help?

Piglet: I learned a lot from Internet drama. That we still need feminism. Twenty years ago on soc.feminism I was writing about how I don't hate my body. We shouldn't get discouraged on the first, fourth, and fifteenth conversations. The point has to be (and will be) made over and over. It did teach me. I learned something.

Vito: Convincing someone else takes time.

Julia: I have learned that I am ignorant about a lot of things. Some of the stuff I've learned... Well, for instance I've learned that I am deeply ignorant about Latino culture and I'm working on educating myself.

Liz: I learned something this week. I was just reading a great article on mock Spanish and its racism and how it reinforces whiteness. I had to reevaluate every time I might have said, "no problemo!"

Julia: Oh! West Wing and the fake country of *Qumar.*

Liz: Isn't that umm Bujold?

Julia: Nope, West Wing. Anyway, I thought, "Oh, well, making up this fake country Qumar is maybe a good way to talk about Islam or issues in the Middle East without attacking a particular country." Then a friend pointed out to me, that the fake country is never some place like France or England? I was like ohhhhhh! now I get it!

Piglet: How do you apologize? Not getting defensive, but to say, oh, you're right I'm sorry.

Vito: What if you don't get that right?

Vito: How not to make a heidipology! Heidi in Harry Potter fandom is famous for her fake apologies.

"I am sorry people are so hasty to trust, and so hasty to distrust in a cyber-world where it is easy to hide, and bully, and not deal with the repercussions of actions. I am sorry if this is taken the wrong way and once again misconstrued."

"I am sorry I have to see hypocrisy."

Liz: We deal with it in other conversations about sexism at tech conferences. For instance, Rubyfail, Perl Playmate fail. It's all documented at http://geekfeminism.wikia.com.

Julia: When someone calls you out, you may not be able to engage right away. You may need to process your defensiveness or hurt first. You can leave a comment that you saw it, you're taking a break and will get back to them.

Vito: What if I don't have time to deal with this? Can you participate if you don't have an hour a day to keep up? How long can you read RaceFail?[1]

Liz: Only an hour?!

Julia: I feel like these things can eat my brain sometimes. I get so frustrated, upset, and mad.

Liz: It's important! Keep up with it, if all your friends are paying attention to some issue then read about it.

Audience: How DO we keep up with it?

Liz: We need whatswrongontheinternet.com and reporters to update it.

Julia: I call that LiveJournal.

Liz: Twitter is kind of good for it.

Vito: Also http://linkspam.dreamwidth.org, http://metafandom.livejournal.com, and http://www.journalfen.net/community/fandom_

1 RaceFail was a long discussion of issues of cultural appropriation, race and racism within published SFF and SFF fandom. For a fuller summary see: http://wiki.feministsf.net/index.php?title=RaceFail_09 or http://rydra-wong.livejournal.com/155427.html

wank, and http://www.journalfen.net/community/unfunnybusiness are all good places to look.

Charlotte: If my sister wasn't keeping up with it, I wouldn't know.

Lisa Cohen (from audience): What about someone like Ian who doesn't read the net, but wanted to get more aware of RaceFail and what people would be talking about at WisCon?

Liz: Zines! Newspapers! maybe we need print magazines about the internet drama.

Print media is already like one-third "something happened on the Internet," but it is very very slow and can't keep up, and misses quite a lot or doesn't cover it because it's too controversial or is about racism, or sex; so when they do it's not gossipy enough to be interesting. They don't know who to interview, and our journals are not legitimate sources. Basically, there are no legitimate sources.

Julia: Well people maybe need to take responsibility for themselves and do something about reading up on things.

Liz: We should all know about the Great Blow Job Wars of the feminist blogosphere.

Audience and panel: (collectively) Whut?

Liz: People are NOT aware of the great blow job wars of 2005,[2] what?! We have lost our history.

Vito: Coffeeandink[3] is sort of a reporter on Internet fail. She is so good: commentary, links, status, and analysis.

~general agreement amongst everyone on this point~

Liz: I've been thinking about Dale Spender's principle that as a feminist I have to show the person I'm talking about what I'm going to say about them, and consider their response and feelings as a human

---

2 http://www.feministe.us/blog/archives/2006/06/19/feminist-politics-of-blowjobs/.

3 http://coffeeandink.dreamwidth.org/.

being. Considering that changes what I want to say. I tried it with Rachel Moss and with theferrett from Open Source Boob.[4]

Audience: What did they say?

Liz: Both of them talked with me and kind of thought about it and declined. Maybe in the future we will get their perspective. It changed how I talked about them.

Julia: So. Seal Press and Amanda Marcotte. Seal Press published her book *It's a Jungle Out There: The Feminist Survival Guide to Politically Inhospitable Environments*. They decided it would be awesome to illustrate the book with "kitschy" pictures from a pulp comic. The pictures they chose were about a white lady in a leopard print in the jungle, pitted against spear chucking natives (no really, they had spears). In one chapter about defending yourself from attack by the religious right, the spear chucking natives represent the threat. The cover also included a "retro kitsch" image of the white blond lady in the jungle.

Vito: Marcotte could have said "Oh, damn I didn't see that. We fucked up." She could have said "I'll think about it and respond." But she chose the third path, which was to say, "Fuck you!"

Julia: Marcotte was incredibly defensive, accused people of being jealous of her, and lacking a sense of humor. Given how feminists are often derided as humorless when they complain about sexism, it's pretty bold of her to make that assertion.

There was also the situation of Marcotte using material without attribution from the radical woman of color blogger BrownFemiPower (BFP) in a published article.[5] Oh and Seal Press busted out some amazing behavior at a WAM (Women Action and Media) conference. When a black female blogger BlackAmazon made a blog post expressing irritation at Seal Press not publishing women of color, Seal Press

4 See *The WisCon Chronicles* vol. 3 for essays talking about Rachel Moss and theferret. Also see: http://theangryblackwoman.com/2008/05/28/what-rachel-moss-did/ and http://geekfeminism.wikia.com/wiki/Open_Source_Boob_Project.

5 http://problemchylde.wordpress.com/2008/04/08/dont-hate-appropriate/.

staff jumped into comments making a series of rude, and unprofessional comments including accusing BlackAmazon and her readers of being rude, hostile, and loud. The defensiveness spilled into their official blog in a series of edited and deleted posts. When a prominent black professor who had worked with Seal Press for decades made a series of critiques, they still took the, "Fuck you," path. [6]

Liz: And I was like dang do I have to not read Pandangon[7] now? Because it's mostly really good.

Audience: What do you do when someone is generally awesome but then they fail? Fail really badly, and they're your guest of honor in two weeks. Just hypothetically...

Liz: We should have spontaneous programming about Mammoth Fail right now![8] Could we handle it?

Julia: The bar for how a con should react officially is low.

Vito: Yes.

Julia: Honestly, all a concom has to do is just not say, "Shut up! You're being too sensitive." How hard is that? Even just saying there are people who have a concern about X, and that the concom has no official opinion on the matter is useful.

Julia: There is a con in Boston called Vericon. They made an announcement about how they were really excited to have Orson Scott Card as their GoH. They somehow missed all the controversy about Card's homophobia, hatred of gay marriage, or all the horrible things

---

6 http://guyaneseterror.blogspot.com/2008/03/notes-so-far-from-wam.html is what started the imbroglio and http://thecurvature.com/2008/04/23/its-a-small-feminist-world/ gives a good summary of what happened. The blogger Professor Black Woman (who had, until this incident, consistently supported Seal Press by using their books in her classes) eventually shut down her blog because of harassment by Seal Press staff. Her blog was at: http://profbw.wordpress.com/.

7 http://pandagon.net/.

8 Mammoth Fail refers to a discussion of problems with the erasure of indigenous peoples in Patricia Wrede's *Thirteenth Child*. Wrede attended WisCon 33. For more detailed discussion see: http://linkspam.dreamwidth.org/880.html.

he said about how marriage equality in Massachusetts was going to destroy the nation. The concom listened to people's concerns, and explained how they would work to minimize further potential problems.

Liz: Why do they fear it! Embrace it! Let people go off! It's conversation! We *want* people to talk about difficult stuff and ideas!

Audience: Sue Jacobi wrote *The Age of American Unreason*. It's a great book, read it.

Julia: Will Shetterly...

Liz: Were you pronouncing the asterisks when you said W*ll Sh*tt*rly?[9]

Julia: Of course!

Audience: Don't say it three times.

Julia: I don't think I could have a really respectful conversation with him.

Liz: What are tools for discussion? Image macros and bingo cards. What about the joy of drama!

Vito: What about when your friend does something wrong to someone you don't like?

Julia: Oh, this is the part where I hate having principles a lot. Say you love them and respect them, and this privilege call out is an act of love and affection. Say: "I don't think you meant to do that, I don't think you're the most horrible person ever, and I'm telling you because I think you can handle it."

---

9 Some people refer to author Will Shetterly as W*ll Sh*tt*rly because, if his name was mentioned in a post about racism, he would show up and derail the conversation in a frustrating fashion. Many of Shetterly's friends at various points have urged him to stop commenting because they felt he was acting in a clueless and disruptive way. Several people have indicated that, unlike in his online interactions, Shetterly can be convivial in person. For detailed information about this see: http://coffeeandink.livejournal.com/881075.html.

Liz: We should keep in mind how it feels to be in that hot seat of having fucked up. It sucks when 2000 strangers are piling on you. I'm not necessarily saying pity them, but know they are shell-shocked a bit. Expect it.

Danny (from audience): What seems to spark a particularly bad reaction is a bunch of people's reactions being called a "mob." It is not a mob. It is a lot of individuals having their own valid reactions.

Liz: You might have to be particularly skilled at ignoring what people say about you, too, to be doing whatever you're doing. Amanda Marcotte has had to develop a thick skin. After dealing with taking fire from actual idiots and being a bit famous, then a person might misapply that thick skin when hearing criticism from allies.

Julia: Let's talk about Vito's problematic panel from WisCon 31 about the "The Master's tools."[10] Also the aggravation of the "tone" argument and it not being OK to express anger. The tone argument being, "If you just said it nicely, then I would have listened. But you were mean so I'm ignoring everything you had to say." Liz, I'm going to pick on you.

Liz: Oh goody! You're talking about ME!

Julia: When I get mad about something like a wheelchair ramp not being in this room so you could get to the podium, I will be seen as more reasonable and polite than Liz making the same statement. "Oh, it's great Julia is so passionate about accessibility for people with disabilities." My anger is okay while Liz's won't be.

Liz: Sometimes that's okay and helpful but sometimes I really don't like it when people appropriate my anger, I'm like: "Go have your own anger about your own issues!"

Julia: Yeah, as an ally, you have to suck it up because sometimes you will fail.

---

10 http://wiki.feministsf.net/index.php?title=But_the_Master_Has_a_Black_%26_Decker_%28WisCon_31%29 and http://vito-excalibur.livejournal.com/140210.html.

Audience: There is a misconception that what we're going for is zero fail. People are scared to fuck up. But people will fuck up! I love to read fail and I love to snark. I don't hope for a fail-less universe.

Vito: I'm going to be a jerk and refer to my own post. I posted a conversation not about David Levine—nice guy, friend of friends—but imaginary David Ravine. It touched on one of my fuck ups, which I won't go into. Do read it, it says what I wanted to express about that.[11]

Bifemmefatale (from audience): I get to where, I'm privileged and I'm not going to post about it, but oh I wonder if I'm harming my friends or POC or trans friends by being silent...

Vito: Interrupting you, with love and affection, I don't care about your guilt. Do whatever you want.

Liz: How do we not burn out?

Vito: Sometimes taking it to protected spaces. Deepa did that with locking some posts after a certain point so random haters couldn't show up.

Julia: There are definitely issues about burnout in progressive communities.

Audience: Shetterly has an internet safe word for his friends now.

Audience: Can we know what this word is???

~everyone cracks up~

Vito: It would not work even if we knew it.

Alan Bostick: There is this horrible, misogynist, racist, etc. community that I have to be involved with for my professional life. I feel sometimes like the only voice of reason in the community, and I'm seen as the asshole.

Liz: Hmm. Cry me a river??

~brief silence in room~

---

11 http://vito-excalibur.livejournal.com/208031.html

Julia: Yeah. You just have to suck it.

Piglet: You might just have to deal.

Julia: OK, let me give you a longer answer. Last year at the "Trans 101" panel, there was this earnest young cisgendered guy in the audience. He asked what he can do to make sure he always gets people's gender correct and never uses the wrong pronouns. He doesn't want to upset people. My response basically was, "you're going to screw up. Suck it up and deal." What I mean by that is he *is* going to make mistakes. As allies we can try hard to be sensitive and aware, but we are inevitably going to trip over our own privilege and face plant. That's normal. What you do next is pick yourself up, figure out how or why you fucked up, and try not to do it again. The idea that you can go through the world without ever being embarrassed or called out is an incredibly privileged position to take.

Liz: [A long serious answer to Alan B. about women in tech conferences, having a guy running a hackathon say "Mars needs women" and me agreeing that more women should attend, but do I want to bring my friends into that situation just to be my back-up, when the situation will be full of fail and harm?]

Naamen (from audience): Back-up and having a community is affirming for me. I can say "was this just fucked up or was it my imagination?" Back-up is not having minions!

Karen (from audience): If you're like, oh, "I feel like such an asshole," keep in mind the "Asshole theory of systems." Every system needs one asshole—it keeps things flowing.

Vito: And if you don't know who the asshole is, it's you.

Liz: There's a danger of being a pet asshole and getting co-opted. The pet radical who makes a community feel like it is tolerant.

Audience: Where you put your asshole is important. Don't put them above you, you'll be covered in shit!

Audience: Suck it up and deal with it is a valid response too.

Julia: Usually when I say "suck it up" I talk to the person about why they need to suck it.

Liz: My friend has a tag for #suckit (QueenofSpain on twitter).

[Liz was not able to capture panelists' closing thoughts except for the following.]

Piglet: And in closing, I just want to refer back to something Julia said earlier: people of color are not a hive mind!

Julia (Starkey) is a geeky, mixed race, fat, queer woman who lives in the Boston area. Julia brings her love of intersectionality to the groups she is involved with. She is a second general sf/f fan who was introduced to the genre by her father. Julia is working on not over-committing herself.

Reflected Self, Refracted Identities: The Meanings of Multiplicity

Allison Morris

Introduction

Clones are an enduring popular trope in speculative fiction, one that crosses media boundaries and appears in a form that is largely unchanged by the more recent development of real-world cloning. The lack of impact that scientific realities have had on the manner in which clones are portrayed, or the sustained popularity of those portrayals, suggests conclusions about why the trope itself is successful with audiences. Differences between real and fictional clones are the essence of what makes clones an attractive cliché; fictional clones can allow a familiar framework for storylines that examine what it means to be unique, the relationship of identity to memory and experience, and, in some cases, a way to look at privilege via a metaphor of what makes an individual valid as a human. Are we replaceable? Would anyone notice if we were replaced? Would we, ourselves, notice? In a less exploratory, somewhat more problematic way, clones also can reinforce an essentialist idea that human potential and personality are reflected in our physical traits and tied to the outward appearance of a given body.

In reality, a fully cloned animal is a genetic twin—an identical twin, but nothing more. The fictional version goes beyond that, including duplicated skills, traits, knowledge, personality, and often the apparent physical age and complete memories of the cloned original.

Farscape, *Battlestar Galactica* (2003), and *Stargate: Atlantis* have all used clones repeatedly in episodes and story arcs, each using multiple variants of the trope while positioning clones both as characters and as plot devices, making those series good contemporary examples that postdate the achievement of real world cloning. They have used those variants of the clone trope to somewhat different ends while carrying out what I believe is a central function of speculative fiction: exploring reality via metaphor. For the purpose of this paper I have found it useful to divide portrayals of fictional clones into three distinct categories: the duplicate body copy, the substitute body copy, and the disembodied copy. All three can be mined to explore ideas of the body as identity, memory as identity, and appearance as identity, noting that the terms "identity" and "personality" can be used interchangeably within those phrases and that they connote fragments of a whole that validates, or fails to validate, a legitimated individuality.

Duplicate Bodies

The first category within this model is the duplicate body. The duplicate is a clone that, in theory at least, has the potential to coexist with the original version and with other copies. Duplicates are often treated as physical (body) spares or living organ farms in books and film.[1] That representation is rarely central to duplicate clones appearing in serial format. Because those stories, with a few notable exceptions, tend to center on the clone as protagonist, the escape narrative that results isn't easily sustained episodically. While the spare bodies that appear in other media may lack their original's memories and identity—functional amnesiacs free to develop their own personas—television duplicates generally have the same memories and experiences as the people of whom they are copies up to a clearly defined, transparently displayed point of duplication, which then also becomes a point of divergence. The duplicate clone can allow division of responsibilities, segmenting of a character's emotional roles, strategies that require a character to be in two places at once, and victory by misdirection and decoying.

In *Stargate: Atlantis*, the duplicate body storyline arises in the season four episode "This Mortal Coil" (2007). In the course of a crisis in the city, the four main characters begin to notice inconsistencies in the world around them and in the behavior of their own

1 Mark Jerng's article allows an interesting contrast in both media source and the spare body clone trope's use in two recent works: the 2005 movie *The Island* and Kazuo Ishiguro's 2005 novel *Never Let Me Go*.

bodies, leading to a discovery that they are hybrid human-robot copies of the people they believed themselves to be. Their memories and personalities are intact and had been allowed to diverge from their originals only slightly over time by means of an elaborate simulation. Following their escape from the false Atlantis, the clones attempt to return to the true city—a home they remember but have never actually inhabited. Contact with their originals leads to an uncomfortable attempt at negotiating a way to accommodate both the originals and the clones within the expedition: this is resolved when the clones are killed while impersonating the "real" characters, allowing the originals to survive.

Where a clear hierarchy is displayed by the lack of question about which team will die in place of the other in the *Atlantis* example, *Farscape*'s use of duplicate clones is a bit more complex. That storyline and its fallout were central to most of that show's third season, beginning with the episode "Eat Me" (2001). Here, three of the main characters are "twinned" by a murdering cannibalistic mad scientist—a procedure that creates two equal, identical copies of a person, destroying the original in the process. The copies of two characters are murdered and eaten immediately, but the show's main protagonist, John Crichton, is twinned in the course of defeating the villain, something that isn't discovered until both copies join the other characters. These clones are particularly interesting because they are explicitly equal, something that's explained in dialog and shown visually by means of an extended synchronized game of rock-paper-scissors—a game that neither can win because they cannot help but to mirror each other. However, *Farscape* extrapolates the likely consequences of slight shifts in the points of view of the two copies immediately, and, as their experiences diverge over the following ten episodes, the two Crichtons become very similar people, but with distinct identities. One of the Crichtons dies, but unlike the *Atlantis* example, he isn't sacrificed in the place of the other, but rather in a plot independent of his twin. His freestanding identity is reinforced for viewers with a reprise of the rock-paper-scissors match during which the surviving clone is unable to anticipate moves while competing with a recording of his late counterpart ("Fractures" [2001]).

Through its worldbuilding, *Battlestar Galactica* is able to use duplicates in a completely different way than the other two series.

Human-form Cylons, robots that are in many ways biological clones, can fit two of the three clone categories, depending on whether they are looked at as individuals or as model types. Looked at as models or lines, Cylons function as duplicates—each copy of a body within a single model shares aptitudes, personality types, and emotional responses despite a lack of shared memory or identical experience. Cylon models are the closest these examples get to the clone-as-organ-farm idea, as their consciousnesses are downloaded into new bodies kept "empty" and ready for use when their current bodies are killed; however, since those bodies are assumed to have never attained any sort of independent function and, in fact, are never shown not animated by a mature Cylon consciousness, they don't quite fit that trope. The Cylon body is a thing, a vessel, until it holds the mind or datastream that makes up an individual. Cylons within each model are, with a few occasional cosmetic differences, physically identical. They are the same apparent age, they dress in a similar (and sometimes identical) manner, they are expected to share the same opinions ("Six of One" [2008]). I would like to propose that each model can actually be treated as a single identity overall in a limited manner, where the model has a single id and super-ego, but each body has a unique and variable ego. Within that framework, the model exists simultaneously in a number of bodies, each a duplicate id/super-ego clone of all.

It's pertinent to clarify that single individual Cylons are, generally speaking, not clones within the framework of the fictional definition that I'm using, as they do not have a duplicated discontinuity of experience when their memories move bodies. There are not generally two Cylons with a single ego shared between them—and the infrequent exceptions to that statement are not duplicate-variety clones, in any case.[2]

Despite their outer appearance as clones, and their admittedly idiosyncratic fit within the duplicate clone category, individual Cylons also function in a manner that is very similar to another enduring science fiction cliché involving look-alikes: the alternate universe

2 The best example of an exception to this is the Eight who has taken on memories from Athena's downloaded consciousness—this unnamed Sharon-model Cylon is, in part, also Athena, sharing a segment of both her memories and her desires ("The Hub" [2008]).

(AU) visitor. Like such characters, Cylons have identical bodies, but their differing experiences make them all very different people.

Substitute Bodies

Where the duplicate clone can potentially coexist with other copies, or with the original from which they were created, the substitute clone is by definition positioned to replace or displace the original. This can happen within stories through accidents of circumstance or due to malevolent outside agendas. Substitute clones may or may not initially be aware of their status as copies, but when they are aware, they are generally complicit in their impersonation of the original.

In the fourth season *Farscape* episode "Bringing Home the Beacon" (2003), the substitute clone is a biological robot copy of main character Aeryn Sun sent to actively infiltrate the ship. The clone hides the capture of the character as well as serving as a tracking device. The clone's true nature is revealed when her memory is shown as incomplete—she lacks a piece of private shared knowledge.

In both *Battlestar Galactica* and *Stargate: Atlantis*, the most prominent examples of the substitute type are not threats to their originals simply because those originals are already dead. In *Atlantis*, Carson Beckett is killed in an explosion during the third season episode "Sunday" (2007). His clone, revealed to have been created months prior to his death and kept prisoner, unaware of his status, is found by the expedition in the late fourth season episode "The Kindred (part 2)" (2008). In *Battlestar Galactica*, Kara Thrace dies when her ship explodes in the third season episode "Maelstrom." She returns to the *Galactica* with no memory of her own death and no explanation for her absence at the close of final episode of the third season, "Crossroads (part 2)" (2007), and discovers the corpse of her original and, by extension, deduces her own nature as some type of clone or copy in the fourth season episode "Sometimes a Great Notion" (2009).

All three of these examples show clones in active competition for their identities, and the three are successful to differing degrees: the clone of Aeryn Sun is killed as soon as she is revealed, the clone of Kara Thrace destroys the corpse of her original to hide her nature and to avoid the questions and increased suspicions that would arise from confirmation that she was not the original Kara, and the clone of Carson Beckett, whose nature is never hidden from anyone other than himself, is able to openly and easily step into the vacancy in relationships left by the death of his original. The differences in the ways that these storylines resolve are strongly related to their motives, the integrity of their memories, and the presence of a physical body with which to compete. Aeryn's copy's discrediting is entirely due to her flawed memory, but her displacement of the original could only last as long as the real Aeryn was kept physically hidden, and, had she been revealed, a struggle for place would have resulted. Kara Thrace's copy's memory is a closer approximation of the original, but becomes vague and untrustworthy prior to the death of her original, and stays vague until she reappears on the *Galactica.* Her uncertainty makes her position with the fleet tenuous, and her lack of definite credible identity compels her to actively destroy the body of her original, removing a potential threat to her assumption of the original's place without making herself any more secure. Carson Beckett's copy's memories are continuous and unbroken. They diverge from those of the original, but are complete and correct up to that point. The original Carson's body has been destroyed, the remains removed entirely from not only the city, but the galaxy as well. And while the copy is unable to resume his professional position within the expedition for a variety of reasons, he easily resumes his original version's emotional and social place within the bounds of his Pegasus galaxy relationships.

Disembodies

The final category of clones within this model is the disembodied clone, appearing variously as neural clones and as artificial intelligence (AI) copies of characters. While some AI, hologram, or hallucinatory versions of characters fit the clone trope, it is necessary to point out that not all do. Within the definitions I am using here, all fictional clones are copies with an inherent duplication of experience but a divergence from the original, which they may or may not initially be aware of, and that discontinuity is important to note in these particular cases, since there are non-clone examples that look very similar to these examples on a surface level.

In *Battlestar Galactica*, the best example of a disembodied clone is a copy of a previously encountered Cylon individual, known colloquially by viewers as Head Six. Head Six is introduced as a character in the initial miniseries, and her character arc lasts the duration of the show. It's left somewhat ambiguous whether she is a hallucination and the product of mental illness, or whether she is an AI program seated in a chip implanted in Gaius Baltar's brain—and it's also left ambiguous whether her origin remains the same throughout the series. My own interpretation is heavily weighted toward the AI and chip explanation, based on her knowledge of information Baltar would not have been privy to, and her apparent and repeated ability to influence outside events. There is a third possibility raised in the show's finale, positing that she is supernatural or angelic in origin—I find that unsupported by the previous text, though that interpretation would not contradict her categorization as a disembodied clone here.

Farscape's disembodied clone has nearly as long a run and as great an impact on his series. A neural clone of ongoing series villain Scorpius, colloquially called Harvey within the series in reference to the 1950 movie of the same name, is created via means of a chip implanted in the series protagonist's brain during the first season of the show. Harvey begins to actually appear in dreamscapes and in waking hallucinations in the season two episode "Crackers Don't Matter" (2000). He survives until the series-concluding miniseries, at which point he completes his programming and shuts down ("The Peacekeeper Wars" [2004]).

The *Stargate: Atlantis* example of a disembodied clone is a single-episode character: the AI version of main character Rodney McKay appearing in the late season four episode "The Last Man" (2008). The McKay clone is a hologram created twenty-five years after the main chronology of the series, activated millions of years into the future to interact with and guide the series protagonist through a crisis brought on by accidental time travel. Within the protagonist's experience and the timeline of the narrative, the AI version is contemporary to his real-world original, though according to a strict timeline, he is active long after his original's death.

Disembodied clones in all of these examples are perfect emotional and experiential copies of their creators up to the point of their creation. They hold outside knowledge that is not otherwise accessible to the character that they interact with, their interactions are tied to a single person, they manipulate the behavior of their target—sometimes emotionally and occasionally physically—and outside proof that they actually exist and are not imagined is the exception rather than the rule. These clones are entirely knowledge based, but the framing of their behavior is reliant on their target's experiences with the original version, making their appearance as a physical copy of their original emotionally resonant and centrally important to their ability to function. These three disembodied clones are goal oriented, but they can and do grow and change over time. In the *Farscape* and *Battlestar Galactica* examples, they can physically manipulate or take over the bodies of their targets for a brief time, moving them through acts that the targets are otherwise unwilling to take part in, and behaving as puppetmasters.[3]

Legitimacy, Memory, and Experience

All of the previously mentioned clone examples are useful in exploring popular cultural attitudes toward what elements make up a valid individual identity. The body and physical appearance are given a secondary position, but still considerable primacy, as a shaper of personality within these examples, in an essentialist view of what creates an individual person. This is arguably most obvious in *Battlestar Galactica* looking at the individuals within each Cylon model. Theory around the philosophy of mind yields a number of useful ideas for translating media reflections of ideas of identity into reality, highlighting the messages about humanity that the clone metaphor carries.

Gilbert Ryle's work proposes two kinds of knowledge, a model that is useful within a look at fictional cloning. The first is the memory of having learned something and not forgotten it, referred to as

3 Harvey takes over Crichton's body, animating him from the inside, several times over the course of the series, notably during the *Farscape* season two finale "Die Me, Dichotomy." In *Battlestar Galactica*, Head Six regularly displays an ability to physically manipulate Baltar, and acts as an invisible outside force to hold him upright and to move him despite his lack of cooperation and attempts to struggle free in "Escape Velocity."

"knowing how." The second is the ability to recollect the past and to recall it, referred to as "knowing that." Within the trope, the first type is shown as inherently tied to the form and appearance of the body. Where clones therefore have a shared "knowing how," their "knowing that" is generally the same up to the point of clone creation, at which time it may diverge completely, or may differ based solely on minor differences in positioning. Both types of memory can be said to shape personality, but only the second creates individuality.

Despite the fact that Cylons are not all the same person from a personality identity standpoint, all bodies within a model are expected to generally agree and to function in concert to carry out larger aims, and particularly to all vote the same way when large decisions are up for referendum. To quote Ryle, "To say, then, that a certain motive is a trait in someone's character is to say that he is inclined to do certain sorts of things, make certain sorts of plans…" (1949, 92). Any divergence in character and philosophical outlook within a model is seen as evidence of two things, both dangerous: an unstable personality flaw in the individual personality of the diverging individual, making her dangerous to herself, and evidence of a potential for a sea change in general attitudes within a model.[4]

Cylons are also a good illustration of the question posed by Elizabeth Anscombe, "How do I know that 'I' is not ten thinkers thinking in unison?" (1975, 58). Anscombe proposed a metaphor for personality in which an identity is made up of many thinkers, each taking on a trait. Are the Cylons, as displayed, inherently an illustration of this question that allows viewers to potentially identify their own compartmentalizations and intersectionalities made fictionally flesh? Where the body is a stand-in for nature in a nature-versus-nurture identity-shaping model, recallable memory is presented as the more important experiential nurture element.

---

4 Caprica Six and Boomer, ostensible Cylon heroes after they made victory over the human colonies and fleet possible, hold outsider status and are both targeted for boxing –a death with resurrection disallowed, meant to segregate a disruptive influence from Cylon society—as a result ("Downloaded"). Their potential for sparking change is realized when Caprica Six and Boomer share their ideas, creating a philosophical shift that causes all Cylons to leave Caprica ("Occupation"), and again, when Boomer sets off the conflict leading to a Cylon civil war ("Six of One").

The occurrence within the clone trope of displays of Ryle's concept of "knowledge that" can be interpreted to mean existence as a real, legitimate person with the right to own that body, appearance, memory, and identity. I would also argue that there is an idea within these portrayals that the original body has the experiences, while the copy imagines the experiences, and that the integrity and completeness of that imagined memory imparts valid individuality and the right to an identity, as well as the ability of a clone to continue to exist.

Descartes went further, separating mind and body into discrete elements, stating, "I knew from this that I was a substance, the whole essence or nature of which was to think and which, in order to exist, has no need of any place and does not depend on anything material. Thus this self—that is, the soul by which I am what I am—is completely distinct from the body and is even easier to know than it, and even if the body did not exist the soul would still be everything that it is" (2003, 25).

Ryle modified Descartes' statements, saying: "A person therefore lives through two collateral histories, one consisting of what happens in and to his body, the other consisting of what happens in and to his mind" (1949, 11). Fictional clones rely on both body and mind for identity, created out of a history that is only true according to perspective, and subject to change.

Contemporary serial scifi television is particularly useful for an examination of the clone trope because its visual storytelling allows the audience to extrapolate differences between copies that otherwise display a very close imitation. In contrast, books require clear descriptive differences between iterations of a given character for the narrative to be understandable. For the viewer, there also may be an attraction to the phenomenon of a single actor portraying multiple bodies, shading very fine performative distinctions to show variants. The serial format also allows revisiting different types of clones within the same universe, making storylines in which those clones may potentially go through a variety of trials and tests to prove their legitimacy and identity possible. On a practical level for my purposes, serial television allows a large body of examples with a limited number of sources.

Works Cited

Anscombe, G.E.M. "The First Person." In *Mind and Language*, ed. Samuel Guttenplan, 45-65. Oxford: Clarendon Press, 1975.

"Battlestar Galactica: Miniseries." *Battlestar Galactica*. Prod. R & D TV, 2003. DVD. Universal Pictures, 2005.

"Bringing Home the Beacon." *Farscape*. Prod. Jim Henson Productions; Hallmark Entertainment, 2003. DVD. ADV Films, 2004.

"Crackers Don't Matter." *Farscape*. Prod. The Jim Henson Company; Hallmark Entertainment, 2000. DVD. ADV Films, 2003.

"Crossroads (Part 2)." *Battlestar Galactica*. Prod. R & D TV; Universal Studios, 2007. DVD. Universal Studios Home Entertainment, 2008.

Descartes, René. *Discourse On Method and Related Writings*, trans. Desmond M. Clarke. London: Penguin Books, 2003.

"Die Me, Dichotomy." *Farscape*. Prod. The Jim Henson Company; Hallmark Entertainment, 2001. DVD. ADV Films, 2003.

"Downloaded." *Battlestar Galactica*. Prod. R & D TV; Universal Studios, 2006. DVD. Universal Studios Home Entertainment, 2006.

"Eat Me." *Farscape*. Prod. Jim Henson Company; Sci-Fi Channel, 2001. DVD. ADV Films, 2003.

"Escape Velocity." *Battlestar Galactica.* Prod. R & D TV; Universal Studios, 2008. DVD. Universal Studios Home Entertainment, 2009.

"Fractures." *Farscape*. Prod. The Jim Henson Productions; Sci-Fi Channel, 2001. DVD. ADV Films, 2004.

"The Hub." *Battlestar Galactica.* Prod. R & D TV; Universal Studios, 2008. DVD. Universal Studios Home Entertainment, 2009.

Jerng, Mark. "Giving Form to Life: Cloning and Narrative Expectations of the Human." *Partial Answers*. 6.2 (2008): 369-393. *Project Muse*. Web. Jan. 18, 2009.

"The Kindred (Part 2)." *Stargate: Atlantis*. Prod. MGM Television; Sci-Fi Channel, 2008. DVD. MGM DVD, 2008.

"The Last Man." *Stargate: Atlantis*. Prod. MGM Television; Sci-Fi Channel, 2008. DVD. MGM DVD, 2008.

"Maelstrom." *Battlestar Galactica*. Prod. R & D TV; Universal Studios, 2007. DVD. Universal Studios Home Entertainment, 2008.

"Occupation." *Battlestar Galactica*. Prod. R & D TV; Universal Studios, 2006. DVD. Universal Studios Home Entertainment, 2008.

"The Peacekeeper Wars." *Farscape*. Prod. The Jim Henson Company; Sci-Fi Channel, 2004. DVD. Lions Gate Films, 2005.

Ryle, Gilbert. *The Concept of Mind*. Chicago, IL: University of Chicago Press, 1949.

"Six of One." *Battlestar Galactica*. Prod. R & D TV; Universal Studios, 2008. DVD. Universal Studios Home Entertainment, 2009.

"Sometimes a Great Notion." *Battlestar Galactica*. Prod. R & D TV; Universal Studios, 2009. Television.

"Sunday. " *Stargate: Atlantis*. Prod. MGM Television; Sci-Fi Channel, 2007. DVD. MGM DVD, 2008.

"This Mortal Coil." *Stargate: Atlantis*. Prod. MGM Television; Sci-Fi Channel, 2007. DVD. MGM DVD, 2008.

Allison Morris works in public libraries because she loves the ways that information, entertainment, and community intersect. That's also why she loves fandom. She maintains the Audiofic podfic archive at http://audiofic.jinjurly.com, volunteers with the Organization for Transformative Works, and is annoyed that despite living in the future sleep is still necessary.

Birthing a Writers' Community

Nancy Jane Moore

Do you dream of living at WisCon year round? Or rather, living at WisCon year round while still getting a reasonable amount of sleep, having the things and people you need for regular living, and being able to retreat to your own private space to rest and regroup.

Have you wanted to take steps to reduce your impact on the environment by installing solar panels or other alternative energy sources, but couldn't afford it? Have you wanted to share useful household things that you don't use all the time—washing machines, gardening tools, even cars—but wanted to make sure the equipment was good quality and that you could get it when you needed it?

Have you worried about how you're going to live as you get older? Or wished you had a handy neighbor who could look after your kids on short notice? Or, for that matter, your cats?

And—especially if you're a writer or other kind of creative artist—have you wanted to have other people like you nearby, people who will understand that you're on deadline, people who will give your work a first read, people who will join you at the rejection letter bonfire? And people who will understand if you don't want to talk to anyone else for a week.

In other words, would you like to live in a writers' community—an intentional community that provides both a good place to live and the intellectual ferment we get at WisCon every year?

Diane Silver and I have been kicking this idea around for the last couple of years and at WisCon 33 we did a panel on the subject to draw more people into the discussion. Michelle Murrain and Monica Valentinelli joined us on the panel.

While a lot of writers have an online community (or communities) these days, the panel was set up to talk about "a brick-and-mortar place that balances private space and time with satisfying contact with other writers and room for public gatherings." Essentially, the core idea is similar to cooperatively owned apartment houses, co-housing projects, and intentional communities of various kinds, except that the residents would be writers and their families. Members of the community would own their own apartments or houses, and would share common space.

At the panel, we focused on barriers to developing such a community, with money presenting the most daunting obstacle. Regardless of whether a group purchased an existing apartment building or bought land and had homes built, up-front development money is necessary. Individuals would also have to come up with some purchase money and be credit-worthy—a particular struggle for self-employed writers.

At the panel, we discussed various ideas for dealing with the financial issues. Certainly, a project could be located in an area where property values are low. Also, there are government and nonprofit grant programs designed for similar projects—a number of cities have developed projects providing studio and living space for visual artists. Another concern we discussed at the panel was how to ensure both compatibility and diversity. The smaller the community, the more important it is that all the members get along reasonably well, and it's easiest to start such an enterprise with a group of friends. But friends can be very homogenous. A good community would reach out to writers of all different backgrounds—ethnic, racial, sexual orientation, gender, class, age, health conditions, etc. After all, one purpose of this project is to support writers, and making sure writers from underrepresented communities are included will contribute to shattering the various publishing glass ceilings.

Besides, while one of the motivations for establishing a writers' community is to live among like people, those "like people" shouldn't be too much alike. Exposure to different backgrounds, opinions, and experiences helps keep us all honest as both writers and human beings.

The panel touched on that constant bugaboo of all real estate discussions: location, location, location. Where should we build a community? Climate, cost-of-living, access to other resources, and our personal favorite places all came into the location discussion, with no immediate resolution.

Though I had one insight as we discussed location: What we really need is not one writers' community, but many of them, a network of them in different parts of the world. They could be small and large, permanent and temporary, some built around publishing, some just around living. This isn't a narrow dream, and it isn't confined to one person or even one group of people. There's more than one way to do this, and everyone is welcome to dream and—even more important—to take steps to turn their dreams into reality.

I'll end this with my personal fantasy. I'd like to take an old building—an apartment house, warehouse, hotel, school, or even an abandoned big box store or mega church—and convert it into apartments of various sizes for about thirty households. There would be lots of common space: a meeting room that would hold all residents, a space for holding writing workshops, an area for exercise classes, and a couple of guest apartments. We'd have lots of green space, and cultivate gardens. In converting the property we'd make it as energy efficient as possible.

We'd have centralized broadband service, with WiFi included to all residents. We'd also have the additional office equipment writers need: copier, high-end printers, postal meter and scales, etc. The community would have good laundry facilities and own a few cars so that members wouldn't have to own private vehicles to get around.

The community would include a mixture of people: single, partnered, old, young, different races and ethnic groups, rich, poor, with different abilities. With luck, we'd have a few people who could provide tech support. Others would be gardeners. Hopefully there would be a few people skilled at home repair.

We could offer an apartment for a writer's retreat, bringing in new people on a regular basis. We could set up a system for selling books online. Perhaps we could even buy POD printing equipment and set up our own print publishing house.

As for where: well, my personal preference is somewhere in the US Southwest, because I like a lot of sun in my life. In or near a progressive city with a good arts and writing scene is also high on my list. Albuquerque would appeal to me, or somewhere near Austin, though in truth I'd probably be willing to sacrifice some of my personal climate and location preferences for a community with a good mix of people.

But I happen to know that there's an old school for sale down in Smithville, Texas, about fifty miles from Austin. Anybody want to join me in figuring out how to buy it and fix it up?

Performance, Gender, and Writing, Continued...

[from Timmel Duchamp in *WisCon Chronicles* Vol. 2]

MJ Hardman

From the first time I ever attended WisCon, at the time of the awarding of the very first Tiptree Award,[1] together with the chocolate typewriter, I knew I had found a home. That is also where I found Elizabeth Vonarburg's *Maerlande Chronicles,* on the short list, a book I have ever since used in my Language and Gender courses. WisCon is also where I became involved in the founding of the Carl Brandon Society,[2] also a home for me in so many ways, not only for myself but also for my husband; we are both now of the Circle of Elders. And, always, every year, I find something else that I can use in my courses, that I can recommend to my students, that I can enjoy myself and that I can use to teach and to stretch the imagination of young ones towards the perception of their own as being of human construction (not an unchangeable given) and toward that which is not yet.[3] I guess we could qualify as "old-timers" but only relatively.

When Ursula Le Guin gave her speech that starts "I am a man" at WisCon 20 in 1996 (later published in *Wave in the Mind*) it felt like meeting a soul mate. Everything she said paralleled something I had also known. And, though I'm not sure this is appropriate to do to a piece of great prose, in academese I have said that it is the very best statement I have ever found as to the deleterious effect of the pseu-

1 http://www.tiptree.org/

2 http://www.carlbrandon.org/

3 If you would like to see those that I have used in this way, on my website http://at.ufl.edu/~hardman-grove/ just below the "Note on the Jaqi Languages" is a list, and also on the left under "Course Summaries" lists can be found under "Linguistics and Science Fiction," "Gender and Language," "Language and Violence," and "Language and Culture."

do-generic masculine. My students have read it every year since, first from my program book and then from the publication—and they do "get" it! It is a most effective statement.

While reading L. Timmel Duchamp's "Creating 'the second self': performance, gender, and authorship" in WisCon Chronicles 2 (2008, 51), I kept feeling empathy with the women she was discussing. Timmi looks at the voices of women writing fiction from what she defines as the onset of the second wave[4] and the many who have stated explicitly that they "wrote as a man" or "wrote to male audiences," at least in the early part of their careers; she also mentions some authors who apparently did not do so; she then comes back to James Tiptree Jr. This article resonated with me in much the same way as Julie Phillips' biography of Tiptree (2006) had earlier. Throughout I kept feeling empathy with what she (or he—Sheldon or Tiptree) was experiencing, even when Phillips herself did not appear to fully understand. I "got" it. I'd been there, done that. The experience in reading Timmi's article was similar but more complicated, as she brought performance into consideration; that our words are, in part, conditioned by the audience, presumed or actual, internal or external. All that Timmi discussed, I believe, is that which many of us went through in order to find our own voices and in order to perform our professions, whatever they be.

Timmi's article, much like Russ's book on *How to Suppress Women's Writing* (1983), addresses itself only to the writing of fiction. I took Russ's book, the categories she suggested regarding agency (Denial of Agency, Pollution of Agency, False Categorization, Isolation, Anomalousness), reified them, and applied them to all areas of endeavor in our culture,[5] with the creative agency of women as the focus. (Partly it is possible for me to perceive these because I also live in a culture where it is not so.[6])

Following up on Timmi's article, I would like to suggest that the experiences, attitudes, and perspectives of the women discussed by Timmi are applicable—like the Russ categories—to all performers:

4 A concept of which most of us to whom it would apply are oblivious, of course.

5 See Hardman, 1994, 2004, and Hardman and Anita Taylor, forthcoming.

6 See Hardman, 1981, 1986, 1994, 1996, 2000, 2001.

performers in the large sense; those of us who speak to an audience in a creative or professional capacity. This was a voice denied to us within our particular historical stream, but so many of us choose not to "behave": many choose to write fiction;-many of us choose another path. Whatever the path we walk our paths cross and recross and we are, I should think, one community in at least a partial sense.

I am an author, but not a "writer"; my hope is that my works *not* contain fiction. I am writing this piece now to continue the conversation that Timmi evoked in what she wrote. Writing is personal, but it also occurs within a social and cultural context that constrains even as it permits. I would argue that that is true indeed of all language, which then touches on the whole of human behavior and experience.

When I applied for graduate school, I sent out some letters that I signed with my full name, some with my initials only, and some with my first initial and middle name spelled out (James). The only schools that replied positively were those that had received letters signed with my initials or my middle name. I guess one could say that I got into graduate school by being a fake man. I even, during those years and into my years as a junior professor, wore tailored suits (but with a skirt; trousers not yet allowed), and a four-in-hand tie. Yes, I was a "fake" man, in many respects, but not enough to buy a house in Florida; for that I would have had to go to court and be **legally** declared an honorary man. Being a "man" was honorary!! In this case "performance," as Timmi discusses it, was insufficient.

In order to publish, one did (and still does in many venues) have to write to/for a presumed white male audience. I also write to a Spanish speaking one, and have been scolded by the administrators of my university therefore: not for the right audience and the writing couldn't, therefore, **count**.

The experiences that Timmi talks about, internal and external, are very like those that I have gone through as I have come to find my own voice, to be able to say what I want/need to say, to produce materials for those for whom I believe they are genuinely valuable (not necessarily white nor academic nor men), to work to change the way in which materials are written in the academy (to reduce the prestige of academese in so far as possible), and to open the doors for those in my classes, many of whom face the same problematical issues of identity as those described in Timmi's article, plus those of race.

In the first full paragraph on page fifty-four (first full paragraph), Timmi discusses the ways in which linguistic/social/cultural roles are reinforced with reiteration (Hardman, 1978), or, as I say in my classes, "day after day, sentence by sentence." I fully agree, and in this paragraph Timmi exemplifies exactly what she explicates (see also Hardman, 1999). Such reiteration can easily override an individual role model, such as Alice's mother; in fact, ridicule and mockery are not far away, and may readily be applied to such models. That has certainly been my experience. Therefore, performing in our own voices requires courage. One of the gifts of my old age is that my daughter has told me so, with admiration. I had never thought of what I have done as requiring courage; her gift of recognition of that courage is for me a treasure.

Timmi closes with a return to the notion of writing as performance. I agree; the audience is there and we adjust our voice to that audience internal and external. And that audience, and our sense of self, is also subject to the whole of our context. And, in these conversations, we are together constructing a context more like that which we would like it to be, as we are audience for each other.

Works Cited

Vonarburg, Elisabeth. *The Maerlande Chronicles*. Beach Holme/Tesseracts Books, Edmonton, AB, Canada, 1993.

Duchamp, L. Timmel. "Creating the 'second self': performance, gender, and authorship." In *The WisCon Chronicles Volume Two*, ed. L. Timmel Duchamp, 51-60. Seattle, WA: Aqueduct Press, 2008.

Hardman, M.J. "Observations for Language and Gender Courses using Joanna Russ." *Women and Language* 17:2 (1994.

———. "War, Language and Gender, What New Can be Said? Framing the Issues." *Women and Language* 27, 2 (Fall 2004): 3-18.

———. "Linguistics Postulates and Applied Anthropological Linguistics." In *Papers on Linguistics and Child Language Ruth Hirsch Weir Memorial Volume*, eds. Honsa & Hardman. The Hague: Mouton, 1978.

———. "Why we should say 'women and men' until it doesn't matter any more" (Guest Editorial) *Women and Language* 22, 1 (Spring 1999): 1-2.

———. *Aymara Language in its Cultural and Social Context*. Social Science Monograph Series, Gainesville, FL: University Presses of Florida, 1981.

———. "Data Source Marking in the Jaqi Languages." In *Evidentiality: The Linguistic Coding of Epistemology*, Vol. XX Advances in Discourse Processes, ed. Wallace Chafe & Johanna Nichols, 113-136. Norwood, NJ: Ablex, 1986.

———. "'And if We Lose Our Name, then What About Our Land?' or, What Price Development?" In *Differences That Make a Difference, Examining the Assumptions in Gender Research*, eds. Lynn H. Turner and Helen M. Stark, 151-162. Westport, CN, and London: Bergin & Garvey, 1994.

———. "The Sexist Circuits of English" *The Humanist* (March/April 1996): 25-32.

———. *Jaqaru*. Germany: Languages of the World/Materials 183, Muenchen, Germany: Lincom Europa, 2000.

———. *Aymara*. Germany: Studies in Native American Linguistics 35, Muenchen, Germany: Lincom Europa, 2001.

———. and Anita Taylor. *Gender & Language: Making the Invisible Visible*, in preparation for online publication.

Le Guin, Ursula. "Introducing Myself " In *The Wave in the Mind*, Boston, MA: Shambhala, 2004.

Phillips, Julie. *James Tiptree, Jr.: The Double Life of Alice B. Sheldon*. New York: St Martin's, 2006.

Russ, Joanna. *How to Suppress Women's Writing*. Austin, TX: University of Texas Press. 1983.

MJ Hardman, Professor of Linguistics and Anthropology at the University of Florida, has been researching the Jaqi languages of Peru, Bolivia and Chile for the last half century, writing grammars, cultural studies and bilingual education materials; a lot of the material is now online. She lives both in Florida and in Peru.
http://at.ufl.edu/~hardman-grove/
http://txupi.wordpress.com/

Getting It Wrong Gracefully
Panel Report

Abra Staffin Wiebe

> Panel Description: There's an antiquated idea among the age old writing tips that an author should only write what they [sic] know. Stepping outside what is familiar is not impossible, not if you really want to make a difference. In the world of spec fic, authors have the freedom to go beyond what they know to create endless possibilities within their fiction. The purpose of this discussion is to not only talk about the logistics of writing about folks unlike yourself, but to talk about how a writer handles the inevitable moment when what you've written offends someone. What to say and what not to say, and in the case where you stumble over your brain and get defensive, something we all are guilty of at one time or another, how to pull yourself back to recover with a sincere apology.
>
> Panelists: Nora Jemisin (moderator), Alan Bostick, Moondancer Drake, Vylar Kaftan, and Mary Robinette.

This was one of the most enlightening panels I attended; it was also one of the most tense—a lot of people went into this already on a hairtrigger, on all sides. The most recent example of "getting it wrong" was RaceFail, so that was the main focus of the discussion.

Personally, I had defensive reactions to some of what was discussed, and I didn't even have a personal stake. I understand that some people will interpret things I say or write as being a certain way because of the color of my skin. It's not fair. It may be prejudiced. But pointing this out or otherwise getting defensive is not a useful reaction.

Apologies

The biggest shocker was that an apology, on its own, is inherently untrustworthy. It's not enough. It has too often been used (by assholes) as an escape clause or a delaying tactic to keep from actually having to change a behavior. If you accidentally offend someone, and you only say you're sorry, *they won't believe you*.

The key is to apologize and then do something about it. For example, John Scalzi bringing POC onto his blog to discuss RaceFail after his initial dismissal pissed people off.

Under no circumstances make a conditional apology. "I'm sorry you feel that way," is particularly to be avoided!

Try not to get defensive. Also, it's never too late to stop being defensive and apologize. Sometimes it's too late for people to believe you no matter what you do, but that doesn't mean you shouldn't do it.

Friends

If something like RaceFail explodes in your online space, you need to moderate your friends' comments to keep them from becoming offensive in your defense, or *you* will be held responsible. (Though apparently defensive friends are the way to go when responding to a bad review [and you shouldn't respond to that yourself!].)

To avoid the echo chamber effect of friends leaping to your defense and making you feel justified, go to the friends who haven't said anything. Silence is *not* support. Ask them, "Am I screwing up?"

Responding

If you don't respond, you're guilty by default. Yeah. Sucks.

Make sure you reconsider and revise your response. Avoid a peer pressure/groupthink response.

Always consider the *worst* way somebody could misinterpret a statement, because that's how it will be taken.

Technique

Try reading your comment/post aloud in the most hateful voice you can, because that's how other people will hear your voice in their head as they read it. If it sounds horrific, reword!

Especially in a big fail, where people actually got hurt, if you don't know or understand the right response, ask how to fix it or educate yourself. *Proceed with great caution at this step.* This can easily provoke the, "It's not my job to teach you," response. It is likely that the offended person has had this conversation dozens or hundreds of times and is tired of it and of how often it seems to not work. A negative reaction may occur after educational resources have already been listed (read the comments!)—maybe even elsewhere, if the fight is being carried on in multiple locations—or when "Teach me how I'm wrong" is seen as a passive-aggressive delaying tactic.

Under these circumstances, perhaps the best response is to post an apology, including an action—or, if there is no clear remedying action, include that you are trying to find resources (if resources have been named, mention them) to educate yourself. Then do that, and mention it later.

There will still be people who do not believe you, and you will probably not be able to convince them otherwise. Trying to may make matters worse at that point.

I find the choice to schedule this panel in the last time slot on Monday interesting.

Abra Staffin Wiebe is a writer of the "a few published short stories, a few unpublished novels" variety. She maintains Aswiebe's Market List (SF/F/H markets and writing links) and runs the Spec the Halls winter holiday contest. Her website is http://www.aswiebe.com, and she blogs at http://cloudscudding.livejournal.com.

My WisCon #5

Isabel Schechter

I am not a parent, but I am a teacher, and I know the pride I feel when one of my students goes out into the world and does something with what I have taught them, and I hope that is what my WisCon friends and mentors feel as they read this essay. They may not agree with me, but they have taught me that agreement is not always necessary, or even desirable, and that sometimes it is the examination of our disagreements that helps us grow, and grow closer.

At my first WisCon, I knew no one. Well, I did know Leah Zeldes for about fifteen minutes. She had been on a panel at Windycon about other conventions and discussed WisCon, and convinced me that I should check it out. That was the grand total of my knowledge about and connection to WisCon. Even so, I bought my membership, made a hotel reservation, packed my bags, told my husband I was taking the car for the weekend, and drove north to the great unknown.

When I first came to WisCon, I was just "some girl." I was ignorant and uneducated in many of the ways of the world, and I knew it, so I mostly just listened and did not contribute, because I was sure I could not keep up with all the sharp, intelligent folks on panels, and all the authors whose work was so beyond me. I had no training in feminist theory, and most of the sf I had read up to that point was by dead white guys. I had never read Joanna Russ, never heard of Suzy McKee Charnas, and had not even noticed that the characters in Earthsea were not all white. I happened to be Hispanic, but that did not really play any active part in my life. If you asked me if I was a POC, I would have said yes, but more out of feeling like it was a technicality, so it was not really an issue in my life.

Even though I was a clueless newbie, just like Ellen Klages said in her GoH speech at W33, when I came to WisCon, I realized that I had come home, I had found my people. WisCon is my safe space. At

WisCon, I am free to be me. I do not have to dress up (unless I want to for the fancy dress party or to wear a costume). I do not have to wear makeup, and no one will judge me based on my looks. I do not have to be professional and proper; I can be silly and giggle and laugh and cackle and snort so hard and so long that I worry I am going to pee in my pants. I am free to just be who I am.

There are also all sorts of wonderful people at WisCon being just who they are. The first year I attended, I felt so welcomed—since I did not know anyone, I had gone to dinner by myself and happened to be sitting one table away from Debbie Notkin and another woman, who saw me by myself and asked if I was alone by choice or if I would like to join them. I had talked to Debbie earlier in the convention, and while she was nice and friendly, I never expected her to invite a stranger she had just met for all of fifteen minutes to intrude on her meal. But that is just how WisCon is (and how Debbie is).

My second year at WisCon, I posted a notice on the WisCon website looking for a roommate and ending up sharing a room with a very nice grad student. The year after that, I brought friends to room with. My friends have now started bringing their friends. We all have it saved on our calendars one year out. We buy our memberships for next year at the current year's convention. We giggle at two AM in our room as we are trying to settle down for the night, only to break out into another giggling fit after about ten seconds of calm. We do all this because WisCon is so much fun.

Giggling with my roommates is only part of the fun, though. There is the Gathering (which I co-chaired for several years), with all its different activities. Seeing people in the hotel lobby and running into them along Main Street—like we own the town! The Clothing Swap. The Tiptree Auction and Ellen Klages! The farmers' market with its wonderful cheese curds! The brunch at Orpheum. The dessert salon and GoH speeches. The outlet mall shopping that happens as part of the pilgrimage to Wisconsin. Staying up way past my bedtime at all the great parties. And so much more.

There is also plenty about WisCon that is serious. It's at WisCon that I learned about feminist theory, oppression, politics, the power of gendered language, cultural appropriation, agency, identity, and so much more. Every year, as it gets close to May, I shift my reading from more casual fare, and start "studying" to get ready for panels. I read works by the GoHs, works that panels are going to be discussing, works by other attendees, and I go back to the lists I collected at last year's convention to be sure I am caught up on all the latest thought so I can participate in the conversation. WisCon is my way to engage my brain in serious thought, to learn and grow.

Over time, I have gone from being a passive observer to an active participant. One year, I complained to Debbie Notkin about a religion panel I attended where the panelists were all religious except for the Jew on the panel, who was secular. I kept seeing that in fandom and wished "they" (the mysterious programming folks) would put some practicing Jews on religion panels for a change. As you can imagine, I was the religious Jew on the religion panel the next year. A couple of years after that, I was on a child-free panel, and the year after that, I moderated the panel. I was also on panels about other subjects. Eventually, I joined the concom and learned all about the mysterious inner workings of this feminist cabal, which turned out to be not so mysterious, but definitely feminist.

And of course, I eventually succumbed to the great and powerful LJ because I could not allow a critique of one child's bad behavior at the convention to turn into a hatefest against all children. (Yep, the childfree person went in to defend the children—that is the WisCon way.) I started out not posting much myself, mostly just commenting on other people's posts and writing convention reports, but that has started to change, both as I have developed friendships that I want to maintain year-round, and as I have become more engaged and active.

I have also started openly identifying as a fan. With each job I have had since that first WisCon, I have made it clear to all prospective employers that I need Memorial Day weekend off to attend WisCon, and that it is a deal breaker. I have even not bothered interviewing for jobs where I knew I would have to work on Memorial Day weekend because missing WisCon is just not an option. I have explained to all my family and friends that no one is allowed to schedule weddings and other celebrations during Memorial Day weekend, and when they have tried to test me by announcing that they think they might have to, the phrase "oh gee, what a pity I won't be able to make it" rolls off my tongue so easily that they realize this WisCon stuff is serious business.

As I have been exposed to sharp, critical people and their ideas, I have started thinking more critically and more deeply about things close to home, like my personal identity. Ian Hageman and Victor Raymond and I had many conversations about my conflicted feelings about the Carl Brandon Society and race issues. Initially, I did not want to have anything to do with an organization that self-segregated or that gave out awards based on race. As time has gone on, I have met some amazing POC, and they have helped me get educated and in touch with a lot of things about myself that I had been trying to get away from or had been privileged by my light skin and economic success to not be affected by, or in some cases, not even notice. The more in touch I got with the parts of me that I had been denying or repressing, the more I noticed how race did impact my life, and the less willing I was to stand back and let it happen. I now actively identify myself as a POC and as a Latina, and I credit that to my participation in WisCon and the conversations that come out of it, including the related conversations on LJ.

However, as I continued to grow and absorb the lessons WisCon taught me about being strong and intelligent, to explore all aspects of my identity, and to speak my mind, I started to notice that all was not as perfect with WisCon as I had thought. Maybe it was always this way and I had just not seen it. Maybe I just was not able to understand it when I saw it. But as time went on, it became more apparent and more disturbing.

Unfortunately, there are some things I do not love about WisCon. The roommate from a few years back who will forever be known as She Who Must Not Be Named, and the annual construction related annoyances on the drive to Wisconsin are not earth-shattering, and so I let them go. Things that are more problematic include being called a "bitchin' babe" by some guy who just met me and thought it was funny, and the fail that includes the now (in)famous Cultural Appropriation of DOOM panel, along with the Racism Inherent in Dwarves and Elves, Romance of the Revolution, Take Back the Sci-Fi, and Getting It Wrong Gracefully panels. The struggle to get a POC-only space this year was no picnic, either. Nor was having anti-religion panels on the program.

These are not panels talking about the very real, sometimes terrible, historical or present-day effects of religion in the world, but panels seeming to say that religion itself was a bad thing. I ran across an anti-religion sentiment a few years earlier, and that is what first made me realize that things at WisCon were not as perfect as I thought. One year, there was a panel about the Religious Left, which was great for me because I got to meet other fans who were also religious and were out doing things in the world that fit with the WisCon way. Things that I could point out to other fans and say "see, we're ok." The following year, we had the panel again and so many people wanted to be on the panel, we could not all fit! It was wonderful. Except for the part where it was clear that we were the minority in the room, and not a liked minority. Not to say that everyone at WisCon is hostile to religion, but it was certainly shocking to be treated as if I were the enemy at WisCon, the place where I had learned to listen to other points of view and respect other people's choices. From the people that are not exactly hostile, I (and others) have experienced being treated like we were trying to force religion down other people's throats simply by wanting to have a panel on it. We are also pitied for being so "willfully naïve" (Are We Done Believing in God Yet?) that we would fall for a stupid thing like religion. In fact, after one anti-religion panel that friends of mine went to this year, they were very upset, and we talked about how at WisCon, it is not acceptable to treat people differently based on a group to which they belong, such as GLBTQ people, differently abled people, POC, media fans, etc., but somehow, it is perfectly acceptable to do so to religious people. I couldn't imagine anyone at WisCon justifying someone using the words "freakish antics" to describe the practices of any of the groups I just mentioned until I saw it listed in the panel description for "Are We Done Believing in God Yet?" It also struck me that "bowing to the social pressure to 'respect' or treat 'seriously' beliefs and opinions which, ultimately have no basis in scientific fact" (We Are the Apes Who Pray) when referring to religion was considered to be compromising. Given that WisCon is a science fiction convention where we regularly talk about things like magic, time travel, and little green men (and women), I was confused as to when scientific proof of something became required before you could discuss it without somehow compromising yourself.

A different disappointment came after the W32 photo nightmare caused by Zathlazip. I waited several weeks for the concom to address the issue and was very disappointed in the response. (To be fair, the concom [of which I was a part] is an all-volunteer organization, and people have jobs and families that have to come first, and there was also the very large Wischolera issue that needed to be dealt with at the same time.) I asked several times during the summer after the convention when we would be issuing a statement about what we were doing/had done, and it seemed like it kept getting put second after the Wischolera issue, which frustrated me. I felt that the Wischolera issue was something that our members would know had been beyond our control and ability to perform any kind of restitution or repair for, that lasted a finite amount of time, and that it could have waited until after the photo situation since there was nothing we could do about it right away anyway. The photo situation, on the other hand, involved the deliberate, malicious invasion of our space, and resulted in our members being terribly hurt, and continuing to be hurt long after the convention was over. It created an unsafe environment, and while I understand that we can never guarantee a safe anything, I felt we owed it to our membership to address the issue and let everyone know what we were doing to try and end it as well as prevent something like it from ever happening again. When it was not really addressed until almost the following year, that was too late. We had had a chance to prove to our membership that we had their backs, and we blew it.

The W32 photo nightmare was not the first time WisCon handled something in less than perfect fashion, unfortunately. A couple of years earlier, there were incidents where people who did not identify as left-ly as the typical WisCon attendee is assumed to be, were apparently also treated poorly. I did not personally experience this, but I saw the hurt that some people expressed at their treatment. I also did not personally experience many of the panels of fail, but I was surprised to be on a race-related panel this year with someone who was known to have participated in one of the panels of fail that dealt with race. Does the programming department not keep a list of people who fail and what panels they should never be on again?

On the other hand, I was not personally affected by two flyers that were placed in the registration packets one year; one which excluded trans-women at a women's event and one making fun of traits displayed by those with autism and Asperger's, but in this case, I was impressed when the concom immediately issued a statement regarding the flyers. WisCon has also done some great things with access issues and made the convention a much less difficult place to navigate for some folks. So, while WisCon is not perfect, it is still the place where I go to each year to exercise my brain and think deep thoughts as well as get my geek on, all while letting it all hang out and not worrying about impressing anyone. There is also still lots of stuff I have yet to experience but want to, like geekaoke, and one year, I swear, I will have a drink (or two) in the bar and go to the dead cow party. I might even make it to the Sign Out one of these years.

I have made known a lot of my feelings to the concom and hope that things will be different in the future. I let them know how I feel because I know from being there that the concom is made up of good people who try really hard to do the right thing. They do not always succeed, but they admit it and try to do better next time. It is the concom's authentic desire to learn and do better that makes it hard so stay angry, even when I feel like I will never be able to calm down and stop feeling hurt. WisCon is still home in many ways, but WisCon has also become bittersweet for me. I know that parts of me are accepted, and that makes me feel comfortable, but unless all the parts of me are accepted, how can I feel fully comfortable?

And so when Ellen said she had found her people, inside, I said, "YES!" and then a moment later, I said "no." Five years ago, I would not have added the, "no." Three years ago, I would not have added the, "no." Unfortunately, I now add, "no." I still say, "YES!" but I also add, "no." You see, for all the Debbie Notkins of the world who invite strangers to dinner and wrangle them onto programming, for all the Jeanne Gomolls who assure newbies that they are competent enough to be on the concom of the world's leading sf convention, for all the Timmi Duchamps who take the time to help grad students come up with ideas for papers, there are also folks that are hostile not just to religion, but to religious people, and who suggest enough anti-religion panels that it seems like there is a track just for that, as well as people who say racist things, or write racist books, or speak down to POC.

At W32, I remember how it felt like my eyes were bugging out of my head at all the POC who attended that year. I am sure there were not more than 20 or 30 of us, and given that WisCon's membership is 1000, 20-30 people is not a large number, but to me, it was huge. I had not realized how isolated I had felt until then. While I had plenty of friends and roommates at WisCon, none of them shared certain core life experiences that were important to me. Not until I was able to go to the "Meeting for those against We-sha-sha," the code title for a POC conversation, was I able to sit and relax and talk to people who understood what I was saying without me having to explain it. When I went to the Can Internet Drama Save the World? panel, I teared up as I thanked all the wonderful POC whose LJs I had been following in the previous year, POC who had brought up issues that made me think, that challenged me, and that let me know that it wasn't just me. I wasn't alone anymore.

And then along came RaceFail '09, which alternately declared that I was not smart enough to participate in the conversation AND that I was over-educated and over-analyzing the conversation; that I was part of a giant orc hoard/hive mind AND that I was part of a rare mythical breed of people that did not really exist because we were all just sock puppets with pseudonyms. And so the marvelous Kate Nepveu created Con or Bust to bring POC fans to W33, and there were so many real, live POC attendees, not only were my eyes bugging out of my head, I am sure my jaw was dropped the majority of the convention. I was surrounded by my people. "My" being all-encompassing for once. My fan friends, my POC friends, my fan friends who were POC!

At our POC Meet and Greet dinner, there were so many of us, we took over a good chunk of the hotel restaurant! I even took pictures of everyone as proof that we really did exist. Along with the laughter, however, someone passed around a letter that the folks that started the Carl Brandon Society had sent to the WisCon concom a decade earlier. It was disheartening to discover that we were still fighting the same battles. It was sad to discover that the battle to create a POC-only space was not something new for W32 that still was not resolved for W33, but was something that had not been resolved back then. As progressive as we like to think WisCon is, sometimes, it's not. The hardest thing about that letter was finding out that folks you thought were there for you, were not; it's one thing to have a stranger treat you poorly, it's another to have people you thought were your friends treat you that way.

Given that we now were a giant unicorn herd (I prefer unicorn to orc, thank you), we at least had each other for back up. So, when we got a text message telling us to go to a panel, we knew there was some monkey business going on that needed to be handled, and were able to offer support and backup. Verb Noire was formed and started publishing, as well as hosting an awesome party. And in keeping with a prior panel at WisCon about starting other feminist sf conventions, Think Galacticon picked up the gauntlet and tackled a lot of the issues that came out of RaceFail and assorted fail that happened at W33.

As an attendee, I had enjoyed WisCon, but had no ownership or stake in it. As a participant, and eventually, concom member, I very much feel that I have both ownership in and responsibility for WisCon. As a member of the WisCon community, I expect and demand that WisCon be everything it taught me to expect from it. I have a right to expect WisCon to be fair and open-minded, egalitarian, and full of opportunity for everyone to participate equally. And, as WisCon has taught me to do, I will call it out when I see it fall short, and demand that it do better.

Participating in WisCon has been one of the great joys in my life. In the decade since I first started attending, I have had several jobs and homes, gone to grad school, celebrated, mourned, welcomed new friends and family into my life and said goodbye to others, and struggled with what I want to be when I grow up. Just like a child learning to ride a bicycle, I feel like I started attending WisCon with training wheels, moved up to riding without the wheels, and can now ride off the path, all because of what WisCon has taught me and been for me. I am looking forward to many more WisCons and to making each of them mine.

An sf reader since childhood, and an active fan for more than 15 years, Isabel Schechter is Puerto-Rican by heritage, Jewish by choice, and vegetarian by conscience. Isabel is also happily married and childfree, and her interests include sf, all things related to food, sewing, and environmental and social justice causes.

WisCon: Happy 10th Anniversary Darling!

JJ Pionke

In light of last year's WisCon Troll, coming to WisCon 33 caused a bit of trepidation for me. For those of you who missed it or don't remember it, the WisCon Troll went around taking pictures of people and then posting them on the internet with derogatory commentary attached, inviting the greater internet community to participate in the derision of con-goers. I seriously considered not coming back. Considering that 33 was going to be my 10th WisCon, I decided that I didn't really want to miss it, and if something happened, it would happen. A lot of bad mojo that goes down tends to be a one time deal, and I bet on that. Luckily for me, lightning did not strike me twice, but still, there was apprehension and I would be lying if I said that I wasn't anxious (and not in a good excited way) about returning to WisCon.

At the end of WisCon 32, I was disappointed with how the Troll was handled by the ConCom. It wasn't until close to WisCon 33 that the ConCom made any kind of announcements about changes to policy or policy clarifications regarding behavior and photography. That it took so long for any real movement definitely made me feel that this was not an issue that the ConCom felt was very important. On the other hand, the ConCom did have to deal with WisCholera from WisCon 32 as well. In the grand scheme of things, an outbreak of serious illness does trump someone, like the Troll, misbehaving badly. Still, this also caused me to be leery of returning and further it concerned me that if something did happen at WisCon 33, the ConCom might not take it as seriously as perhaps it should be taken.

Those of you who know me personally know that I am a great proponent of the underdog and typically, if I see an injustice, I am going to say something about it. This trait makes me a great union leader, and it also gets me into a lot of trouble. Still, despite these very real concerns, I have, typically in the past, had a great time at WisCon, and at this point in my WisCon going life, I know a lot of people there. I wanted to see them because if nothing else, WisCon is about people. There are varying degrees of drama every year, but quintessentially, WisCon is about sharing ideas, getting excited about all the nerdish stuff that mundanes don't understand, staying up too late, not getting enough sleep, and talking to con friends that you haven't seen or really talked to since the last WisCon.

That said, WisCon 33 was definitely more low key and there was a noticeable lack of people taking photographs and recording video of panels or funny moments. This made me rather sad, and then angry all over again that people felt they had to restrict their shutterbug tendencies because of one person from last year. The mood of the con was subdued to say the least. I think more than anything else, people were tired, a bit nervous over the Troll and WisCholera issues from WisCon 32, and there was a definite effort by all to be as drama free as possible. Not that drama didn't happen, because of course it did, but at least it was drama of the intellectual kind rather than the vomiting and libelous kind. Will I continue to return to WisCon?

Yes, definitely. It's my con. It's the con that I look forward to at the end of the school year. It's the con that I travel to, a day or two after I submit final grades. I flee the state of Illinois and go North to MadCity for a weekend away from the devastation left over from the semester. I go to WisCon to see friends, to talk about the things that ***I*** want to talk about, like *Battlestar Galactica*, and to recuperate mentally from a semester of teaching college students that the five paragraph essay is NOT acceptable in college. I love WisCon. There might be ups and downs, but in the grand scheme of things, I've been in a relationship with WisCon for 10 years now. There have been great moments, there have been awful moments, but you don't just walk away from that kind of long-term relationship because something craptastic happened one time. If my WisCon experience had been consistently negative for a few years, I might be singing a different tune, but as it is, it hasn't. I am looking forward to the next 10 years with WisCon in my life.

Happy 10th Anniversary Darling!

JJ (Pionke) teaches at two community colleges in the Chicagoland area. She enjoys riding her motorcycle, reading, and contemplating her next tattoo.

We See What You Did There: A Group Chat among Various POC Who Attended WisCon 33.

Participants: Isabel Schechter, Johanna, Julia Starkey, and K. Joyce Tsai

This piece represents a compilation of dialogue that happened in a group chat online and in email afterwards, edited together by Julia Starkey. Johanna's contributions were added later because she currently lives in the UK, and she was unable to participate in the group chat. Isabel was not present for the beginning of the chat.

Previous Panels Casting Shadows

Joyce: So, WisCon as my WisCon... I didn't really feel like WisCon was my WisCon until I connected more with the horde [note: some groups of POC fans began referring to themselves as "the orc horde" or "wild unicorns".[1]]

Like, the first year I was there, I clung to Yoon and Micole and felt completely outside of everything. And then there was the great "cultural appropriation-debate-of-doom!" panel and the later fallout online, which made it REALLY feel like not my con.

My first year had the cultural appropriation panel of DOOM. My second year the horrible Revolution panel. My second year I had a giant chip on my shoulder and was like, well, the internet is going to yell at me about this anyway, so I might as well go all out. I also remember POC at that WisCon32 saying they came specifically because of the cultural appropriation debate and how grateful I felt.

1 For more information, see http://community.livejournal.com/deadbrowalking/357066.html.

Julia: I think I first found your blog[2] by reading about the cultural appropriation panel. I just reread your essay on "On the 'Romance of the Revolution' panel at WisCon 31" (*The WisCon Chronicles* vol. 2) and was so angry about how that panel went down. I really appreciated that Timmi took responsibility for her part in that.

Joyce: I almost feel as though my response to "Romance of the Revolution" wouldn't have been taken as seriously had Timmi not taken it up. Which I am grateful to her for! But it's also...whose voice gets heard more?

My piece was full of expletives and allcaps and all the things that make you look "irrational" and "shrill."

Julia: It's completely depressing to have your voice be ignored unless a white person approves it. The white person is some how completely neutral in discussions of racism. Even when they admit their complicity.

Joyce: Do you know how scary it was posting stuff like that AND being a complete newbie to the con? And having relatively well-known reviewers like Paul Kincaid going on about how he didn't really mean it blah, blah, blah. I almost feel like it was never my con in the beginning, because I burned all those bridges before I even had them.

And then orc hordes appeared! and I started talking to Carl Brandon Society people! and...it felt more mine then, not entirely, because it was so obvious that it was only a part of the con, you know? But at least there was some space and it helped to have Timmi put the "Romance of the Revolution" write up in *The WisCon Chronicles*, to have it there in the official timeline.

Julia: We aren't "allowed" to be shy, nervous, etc. Also we don't have any fears about being glared at or harassed by the many WisCon members who have been extremely hostile in discussions of race both online and offline.

Johanna: I don't know if I'll ever go to another cultural appropriation panel at WisCon! The two-part one a few years ago—the first part, where the panel just discussed things & it was only open for

2 http://oyceter.dreamwidth.org/.

questions at the end, went really well, because white people in the audience were prevented from derailing, weeping, and whining. The second part was heinous. I should've been clued in by most of the POCs in the audience for part one sneaking out & tons of white people, who hadn't been to the first part, filling the room. I thought it was really interesting & hopeful that there was a cultural appropriation 101 class this year—though I definitely didn't want to go sit in it. Some people have the patience to put up with 101-level fail repeatedly: I'm not one of them! Also, I totally have a mental list of panelists to avoid because I think they're racist jackasses, but don't we all?

Is WisCon an experience of coming home?

Julia: I was thinking about how WisCon is supposed to be this big homecoming (hence The Gathering). Yet POC are not feeling that.

Joyce: I feel a lot of us go prepared for fail. We don't go as a homecoming. We go like we're preparing for battle

Julia: This year I feel like we were more explicit in advance about it being a battle. With all the pre-con organizing, and making sure to show up for each other's panels. And having the horde at my back was just so fucking good. And also knowing that if I couldn't back up someone, there were others who could.

Joyce: That actually helped for me. Like, I felt I could do my own thing more because there were more safeguards in place. And having the time and space to debrief after panels.

Julia: The debriefing was critical because sometimes I ended up going "Did that really happen? Did that person really say that to my face?"

Joyce: It was great for learning about what went on in panels you weren't at.

Julia: And it's amazing to have people say, "yes it did happen," instead of saying, "oh you're over sensitive" and mean, getting, "yes that was fucked."

Joyce: "Yes it did and it was just as bad as you say!" Exactly. It's a reconfirmation of your pov.

Julia: As feminists, I feel we talk a lot about believing women. Except for WOC.

Johanna: See, the thing is, I totally have started feeling like WisCon is a family reunion (after having been to six now), but a lot of that has to do with the orc horde. I do have white friends that I see there & that I love, but without my fellow POCs I think when the inevitable fail happens I would feel even more alienated than I still sometimes do at the con. I love love love the POC meetups, especially the one at the start of the con, because then it does feel like coming home. Also I love sitting around in big POC groups making white people nervous. HA HA.

First WisCon Experiences

Joyce: I remember counting my first WisCon and getting numbers that weren't so great and it was WisCon 30 so Chip Delany and Nalo and etc. were there as GoHs. There were approximately 15 Asians, and 6 Black people in my completely not formal count for WisCon 30. I probably didn't count a lot of native people and Latina/o people.

Julia: My first WisCon was interesting because I was terrified. I am shy and have social anxiety. I was worried no one would like me, I would have nothing to say, and that I would feel isolated.

I walked in and everyone stared. Then, about 15 minutes later, while volunteering, I ran into two smart and hilarious black queer people. After an hour hanging out with them, I was on board with WisCon. Then later that evening they had someone yell racist slurs at them on the street [Note: see Jackie Gross' essay "First WisCon 2007: A cabal of one's own" in *The WisCon Chronicles* vol. 2.]

Joyce: I feel like I keep coming back because more people from the horde keep going, and I feel somewhat guilty about that, because I know a lot of people from the horde go specifically in response to fail. So I feel as though I am benefiting from massive fail.

Julia: My first WisCon is where I met Johanna and had this great grumble fest during a panel about mixed-race people in SF/F. We were both frustrated by hearing people talk about us as if we were tragic mulattos, symbols of the end of racism, or the race of the future, as opposed to actual people with opinions about our identity.

Joyce: I remember she and I were part of the handful of POC who sat through the second part of the cultural appropriation panel (the, ugh, moderated part). And being so glad to have someone there who was saying a lot of the things I was thinking.

Johanna: During that second part of the cultural appropriation discussion a few years ago, I was so incredibly stressed out by what people were saying & how the discussion was being handled that I ended up speaking up more than I really wanted to, but more and more I'll just avoid the discussions. Because it is just too painful.

Julia: And also Nora's post about how she is pulling back from talking about race publicly out of concern for her writing career.

Johanna: My first WisCon was actually in 1999, & I went alone & roomed with random people off the Feminist SF/F mailing list & I didn't really meet anyone because I was shy & totally intimidated. Also, that was before LiveJournal entered my life (& the life of many WisCon folks), ha ha.

When I went back years later with some friends, it was amazing, but as I started getting more conscious of race & racism, it did change the con & what it felt like for me. I love seeing the POC numbers shooting up (well, in relative terms) though, & getting to know more awesome & incredibly smart POCs has been a large part of what's made me keep going back to the con.

Before this year, in particular, due to RaceFail I felt unsafe coming to the con. I checked with other POC WisCon regulars to see who was going & I really did feel like I was bracing myself more than usual. I even considered not going, because I had seen so many WisCon regulars (including lots of BNFs & authors) be so hostile & so high on their white privilege. I thought, well, maybe it's not the place for me after all—this con that I held up over all other cons I'd been to, pretty much the only con I had any interest in attending regularly (well, I hope someday I can go to Think Galacticon too!).

Isabel joins chat.

Isabel: Yeah, I've been thinking a lot about "My WisCon." Normally, it feels very much mine, but this year, not so much. Which is weird considering that I've been coming for so long and I've developed some good friendships, and now even finally have a unicorn herd to belong to.

Julia: Do you think any of that is due to your race/ethnicity? I know we've talked about how people don't realize you are a Latina.

Isabel: The less identified I was as a Latina, the more I felt like I belonged. As I've become more identified (both by myself and by others), I've felt less belonging. Although walking around as part of a visible group, I felt like, yeah, we belong here, this belongs to us!

Joyce: Interesting! I feel like... I belong to a group that's kind of part of WisCon, but not "official" WisCon, almost. Not sure if that makes sense, but I think some of that is because I got stuck in RaceFail my first year there and never found a circle of friends there who did fully belong.

Julia: Yeah. I've been thinking about choosing to identify as a POC and being politicized around race (in the way feminists are politicized around gender). In my experience, doing so will burn bridges with some white people and leads many to treat you differently due to their own discomfort/anxiety about race. Sometimes it feels like, why do that? Why not settle for being considered almost white? But self hatred is a slow poison and tepid acceptance doesn't compare to both self love and the amazingness of the unicorn horde.

Joyce: Exactly!

Isabel: Amen!

Julia: Being with the horde reminds me why I engage in anti-racist activism. It's helping my community stay strong.

Isabel: I agree about the "unofficial" feeling and the amazingness of the unicorn horde. And I struggle with the activism and the cost of it.

Joyce: And it's also been odd watching Micole become more politicized, because even though she is a Nice White Lady (tm), even she gets more ostracized for speaking up, I feel. And it's like, if that's the cost for allies, how much worse is it for us?

Julia: Yeah. I think some of the anger directed at her comes from her betraying whiteness. Like, how dare she point out white people benefiting unfairly from privilege!! She can't be doing it because she thinks it is right, she must have ulterior motives.

Joyce: I feel the past two WisCons I've been engaging less with activism that involves educating white people because I'm so tired. All the hate being directed at you is so exhausting.

Julia: It is like emotional vampirism. They want you to be their unpaid therapist. Go to rent-a-negro.com if you want that.

Joyce: I remember after the "Romance of the Revolution" panel, I was having a hallway conversation with Vito Excalibur, and some random white guy stops us and a) puts his hand on my shoulder and b) proceeds to talk at us for what felt like hours.

Julia: This year several POC also got physically cornered by white guys who wanted to talk at them.

Isabel: This year was an experience in being out there on the concom for me in that I was hyper aware that I was always bringing up stuff or speaking out on it, and I felt like I became the official POC spokesperson or something. And it was really hard for me because I don't really feel qualified to be the official POC since I've only been really working through some of this identity stuff for a couple of years.

Julia: I'm glad you were there bringing stuff up, but I'm sorry that it had to be all on your shoulders. I feel the same way when people treat me like some sort of expert on racism. I'm trying to educate myself, and I'm using resources most people at WisCon have access to.

Joyce: I feel like just the number of POC still makes a difference from con goers to people on the concom. It can either be "token POC voice" or "lots of POC voices and lots of experiences."

Isabel: To be fair, there were allies speaking up too, but there are not a lot of POC on the concom. Nora jumped in a couple of times, and I hadn't known she was on the list. Just knowing I was not alone was very helpful.

Joyce: Do you think the concom did a lot of stuff differently this year?

Isabel: I think the concom is made up of some really great people and they try really hard to do the right thing. And they usually get it, and when they don't, they're open to admitting that they don't and try and fix it That said, there's still some education that needs to happen. And at least one person on concom who...I'm still not sure I've processed how I feel about the things this person said and what an obstruction they were to the POC only space.

Joyce: I wondered how big of a battle it was to get that POC-only room, because I remember the shenanigans from last year when tempest wanted to do POC-only things.[3]

Isabel: Basically everyone but this one person was on board, especially once Jeanne Gomoll, explained that it was similar to feminist women-only spaces back in the day, it wasn't so much a battle as it was an annoyance. This person was really vocal in their opposition and it was *really* upsetting.

Julia: It's such a gut punch to have someone you've spent time with, who you think you are in a community with, be so invested in preventing you from getting something you need.

Joyce: Also...I don't know. I feel like it is awesome having the concom do things and be inclusive to POC. But there's also a big onus on the congoers as well. Like all the fishbowling and ogling and getting Tempest and Julia mixed up and etc. So even if the concom is perfect and welcoming, WisCon can't ever entirely be our con if the people going think we are not a part of it.

Isabel: Argh! I'm still boggled about how people could get Julia and Tempest mixed up! People! We don't all look alike!

---

3 See http://community.livejournal.com/wiscon/127583.html?thread=759391#t759391

Johanna: I appreciate that the concom seemed to make more of an effort this year as far as welcoming POCs & making sure we had some safe space (which was later violated, naturally!). I mean, WisCon tries harder than any other con I've been to, and I appreciate that a lot. But it makes it more frustrating in a way when bad things do happen, because it reminds me of how far we still have to go. And if this is one of the best cons as far as diversity & its community can still fail so much?

There was that piece by Lawrence Schimel in *The WisCon Chronicles vol. 2* that says basically, "WisCon is being diluted by a new focus on stuff like race & class! Will WisCon return to its feminist roots or continue to be diluted by this other crap?!" That was a big pile of are-you-fucking-kidding-me! I saw a con report this year that said something similar, that the con was less feminist, more "diversity and special groups"-focused. This is the problem I have with white people's feminism! (or one of the problems...)

Panels & Parties & People

Julia: One thing I enjoyed was seeing POC on panels that had nothing to do with race. It sends the message that we're not just here to do education for white people. We're here because we're fans and feminists. We are valued members of the community and deserve to be treated as such.

Joyce: Yes! I love whoever came up with "not another @%%$^ race panel."

Isabel: I'm soooo bummed I missed that panel! I will never host another party again if it means I will miss the evening hilarity.

Joyce: Me too!

Joyce: Having Verb Noire at WisCon this year: SO AWESOME! I think that helped a lot making it feel like "mine," because it wasn't just lots of POC fans and a few POC professionals. WE HAD A PRESS!

Isabel: Yes. Verb Noire was awesome! Not only were the unicorns all gathered, but we're all important now that one of us is a PUBLISHER!

Joyce: YES! And they had a party, and despite some dubious behavior by other members, it was more official space for us!

Joyce: And we got Nice White Ladies™ to steal us beer from the Tor party MUHAHAHAHAHA.

Isabel: Yes, there was a lot of great stuff this year. I don't want to give the impression that it was all bad. The unicorn herd effect was awesome.

Julia: I feel like more white allies were realizing they should speak up and do some of the heavy lifting.

Joyce: Being on a panel with Diantha Day Sprouse and Andrea Hairston was AMAZING and getting to talk to them a little after and fangirl them. My mom is super conservative in basically every way imaginable, so being able to talk to WOC from an older generation and learn was SO AWESOME.

Julia: Talking to other generations of feminists makes me so happy. When I realized Nisi Shawl brought her mom, and introduced me to her, I almost started crying.

Joyce: I also loved Jackie talking about her experiences with feminist movements. I am still thinking a lot about defining safe spaces and what Jackie was saying about that.

Isabel: She is one of the lights in my life. She makes me think.

Julia: The last 3 years I would leave WisCon with Jackie's words bouncing around my head, and come back the next year thinking, "Oh yeah I have that figured out!" Then Jackie would nod, go, "Mmhmm. Did you consider XYZ?" and I'm like "Uh…no I didn't. Shoot. Next year I'll have it down!"

Joyce: Yes! I am still thinking a lot about defining safe spaces and what Jackie was saying about that.

[In email Jackie gave a summary of her thoughts on safe spaces: It's important to define space in order to get clear on what it is you are thinking about and/or working on. Or, better yet, airing the "dirty laundry" that may exist, especially between groups of POC. I think people have a tendency to think safe space is a way to make everyone agree, to which I can only laugh.]

Julia: And of course we can't forget how hilarious Jackie is.

Julia: Naamen is such an amazing feminist man. He is so respectful of the space.

Isabel: And can I say that I was so awed by the grace and intelligence that exudes from Deepa that I was awed into silence.

Joyce: Omg I fangirl Deepa so much. I was like, Deepa needs to be on every panel ever! Along with Naamen.

Julia: But here is the other thing about Deepa. I felt so happy she was there. But I was also really sad about the toll RaceFail has taken on her.

I both wanted to talk to her about race, gender, fandom for hours, but I also wanted to have a less intense conversation about books and TV shows we adore.

Joyce: I'm also reminded of what she was saying on the Transformative Works and Cultures write up[4] about how fans keep paying the cost, and it's people who didn't sign up to do it, are doing it on their free time, and etc.

Johanna: There's often such a huge emotional & social cost in calling someone out on racism, even among supposedly progressive people like WisCon attendees. The push-back that people get for bringing that angle up sometimes results in me doubting myself and not raising my hand in a panel, because I start to think that maybe somehow I am taking things too seriously! Which is totally ridiculous, but there you go—yay for internalized racism. Even if I know something wrong just happened, it is so tiring to have to explain over and over to people (and then possibly have to deal with being cornered later

4 http://journal.transformativeworks.org/index.php/twc/article/view/172/119.

in the con, like others have described!) what was wrong about what they just said.

White people don't usually stop and go off to think about what you just said, they feel like you owe it to them to explain repeatedly, in great detail, how they messed up. And then you owe it to them to listen to their tedious explanations about how you don't know what they're talking about or you misinterpreted them or they didn't mean any harm. YES EVEN WISCON PEOPLE. And I agree with how shocking it is that white feminists will use the same arguments that men use to dismiss women in order to dismiss people of color. I mean, how do you not see that you're doing exactly the same thing?

The effects of online racism discussion on WisCon

Joyce: Back to my WisCon. How do you guys think RaceFail[5] had an effect on how the con felt like yours or not?

Isabel: RaceFail definitely had an effect.

Julia: It had an effect, but I wasn't worried about the biggest offenders in that imbroglio. They acted so poorly, I have written them off completely. I have no interest in engaging with them. In my apartment, I moved the books by various offending authors to the "Orson Scott Card Memorial Fail Shelf."

Joyce: I was a little scared of going and meeting a giant wall of supporters who would be hostile.

Isabel: I was more worried about the authors' fans than the actual authors. I also worried about the folks who didn't repudiate the author. What were those people going to be like?

Johanna: I totally agree. I was more afraid of rabid fans than fallacious authors themselves!

Joyce: And I'm still disappointed in the pro communities' overall lack of comment on their peers' behaviors. And I feel like how can WisCon be really our con if the pros frequently aren't talking about

5 http://wiki.feministsf.net/index.php?title=RaceFail_09.

the same things we are? If they're just like, "Oh, Will Shetterly, he's weird online but fine offline!"

Julia: Many of the major RaceFail people have pull due to being published, having a big fan base, having lots of blog readers, etc. etc. And I'm "just a fan."

Joyce: I think there is a lot fans can do. Esp. in light of the *Liar* cover issue.[6]

Isabel: Julia, never say "JUST" and "a fan" in the same sentence! We fans have the power! We buy the books! We vote for awards.

Julia: You're right, Isabel. I just feel like, that published authors with fan bases, have more social capital, more people backing them, and more pull than me.

Isabel: I think a lot of that is because we let it be that way.

Julia: That we let our power get taken from us?

Isabel: I always hear complaints about the pros being elitist in their Governor's Club. Yet does anyone ever talk to them and say, dude, I buy your books, I want you to come downstairs and socialize, dammit!

Joyce: But I think there are still gatekeepers when it comes to how easy or hard it is to turn pro, and whose voices are weighted.

Julia: It's weird because on a certain level I don't give a shit about if someone is a pro or not. Either they have interesting things to say or not. I'm not going to let someone's fame keep me from disagreeing with them. On the other hand, I know that the reaction from people around me will be "oh how dare that nobody say that to such a distinguished person."

Isabel: It is so liberating to know that I can say whatever the hell I want and my book won't suffer since I don't have a book to worry

6 Justine Larbalestier, the author of *Liar* blogged about how her publisher, Bloomsbury, white washed the U.S. book cover. *Liar* is about Black teen with short tightly coiled hair. The original book cover showed a white woman with straight hair. Larbalestier's blog post is at http://justinelarbalestier.com/blog/2009/07/23/aint-that-a-shame/.

about You know, my list of fools to avoid (or make accidentally fall down the stairs) is *getting* larger as more people show their asses.

Joyce: It's amazing how people keep doing it too! You'd think after someone says, "You are making a fool of yourself," they would try to stop, but nooooo...

Isabel: Is it wrong that I don't care about little ole me daring to go up to some jerk and saying, dude, you're a jerk!

Julia: One thing I've noticed is as we're having more interesting and complicated discussions about race, white people are feeling really free to say ignorant things.

Isabel: Why are we so nice to pros who are jerks just because they're pros?

Julia: I think women are socialized to be "nice" and not cause a fuss.

Joyce: Women are socialized to do it, POC are socialized to do it, etc., fans are socialized to not be mean to pros.

Isabel: I say we get over our socialization. I mean, I was socialized to be subservient to a man who would rule over me and to bear him many children...and instead, my husband identifies himself as MY plus one, and we're happily childfree—nothing could be further from my socialization.

Isabel: Why is it that at a feminist convention, no one blinks at being told they have to give up their sexist ideas, but freak out when the same thing is said about racist ideas?

Joyce: But I think there's also the struggle between not giving away power and having to fight to grasp that power from the people who refuse to give it up.

Isabel: I think it's harder to grasp additional power when you give up the power you start with.

Joyce: At the same time, we should not have to fight for every single tiny freaking inch, especially when so many of us get hurt doing it.

Julia: The people who are trying to take power away from us need to be accountable too.

Joyce: We should have the power to call people out on panels and to tell them individually when they are acting fools. But they should also be accountable for being racist.

Isabel: Can we write a manifesto? Things like, X is not acceptable. Neither is Y. You will treat me with respect.

Joyce: Like the Carl Brandon Society rules of discourse!

Julia: Someone having yellow penalty cards/flags. When someone does something racist you wave a yellow flag and they get a foul. Or holding up a sign in back that says "THAT WAS RACIST."

Joyce: And I am so tired how even that gets debated by all the concern trolls going on about, "OMG but then innocent white people will be called racist by cruel POC!" I still think we should pass out bingo cards.

WisCon and Other Cons

Joyce: Since WisCon is the only con I go to, I wanted to ask you guys how much you feel like WisCon is your con compared to other cons?

Julia: So. In terms of other cons I go to, WisCon is the only one that remotely feels like home. There are three local big cons: Arisia, Boskone and Readercon.

Joyce: Ahahaha. And now we all know about how bad Readercon is!

Julia: Having a feminist view point, anti-racist view point, etc. is dismissed out of hand as "PC nonsense." I feel stared at. I feel like people don't believe I belong there. I've been mistaken for cleaning staff repeatedly. It's a nightmare. On the upside, the cleaning staff always loved me. Because I was polite to them and treated them like people. When I wore my glitter Wonder Woman costume, the cleaning staff dragged friends from other areas over to look at it. When I took it off one cleaning person was super sad since she had missed me wearing it. So I put it back on so she could see.

Isabel: That's great, but what does it say that you were relating to the cleaning staff and not other people at the con!

Joyce: My first con was Noreascon, in which I was one of three (3) Asians out of literally THOUSANDS. Asian #2 of 3 was Yoon! Who I went with!

Isabel: Each con I go to, I go to for different reasons. Some are purely about the geeking out and going to parties and dressing up, some are about the deep thinking like WisCon. Each feels comfortable for different reasons. The two that feel most like home are WisCon and Think Galacticon. I have more baggage with WisCon.

Johanna: I've been to several other general sf/f cons, though WisCon is the only one I go to regularly. They are all much worse in terms of diversity & general political fail. I went to Worldcon when it was in Boston a few years ago & I felt really really non-white (and really young). I used to go to a number of anime cons, & they do tend to be more diverse—there are loads more POCs & sometimes there seem to be more women (like I went to every Shoujocon & it isn't surprising that there were lots of women there). But I stopped going partly because of the nauseating level of racism & sexism I saw going on.

Julia: What is particularly crazy-making about Boston area fandom is that I know a good chunk of people on concoms, as well as other "official" people, con regulars, etc. Despite being somewhat "in the know" I'm treated as a clueless newbie.

Isabel: And let's not forget that no one should be treated as a clueless newbie, even the clueless newbies.

Julia: Also many of the people I know are drowning in aversive racism. If I bring up a problematic incident about race, they leap to tell me they are not racist and explain how the racism wasn't racist because we live in Boston (don't they remember the busing horror show that happened in Boston during the 1970s? There were widespread protests and many white parents refused to send their children to majority black schools. The protests were often violent, some becoming riots, and several people died. The ramifications of this fight are still felt over thirty years later.). Anyway, since I can't prove the incident was racist, I should be nice and not bring it up. Most of my local geek friends think of Arisia as a second home. They eagerly wait for it, and have a lot of positive emotional investment in it. For me it's more meh. Especially after being to WisCon.

Isabel: When it looks like racism, and sounds like racism, why decide it might not be racism? How are they ever going to get better if they don't get feedback?

Julia: But Isabel, they know they're not racist. I'm their black friend!

Joyce: You're totally racist for just bringing it up!

Isabel: One thing that Think Galacticon did was define terms before the con.

Joyce: Awesome! How did defining the terms work out?

Isabel: I think it was very helpful. We defined terms and gave out links to educational resources. We also were very clear what level of discourse and type of behavior we expected.

Isabel: I love my Think Galacticon folks. Here's how awesome they are: when the Race Fail shit first happened, I was still shellshocked, and before I could say anything, one of the white people on the concom sent out an email to the list and said—Hey! Have you seen this? What are we going to do? How fast can we do it?

Joyce: OMG that is AWESOME.

Isabel: They were totally there for me, were absolutely appalled, and sprang into action!

Julia: I swear to god we ask so little. Just saying, "Oh look, there was a problem," makes me thrilled to bits.

WisCon Past and Present

Joyce: I always feel ambivalent about WisCon, because it does try and things have been getting better imo. But there's also stuff like the letter by POC WisCon members from TEN YEARS ago,[7] and how much fail there still is

7 This letter is reprinted in this volume of the *WisCon Chronicles*.

Julia: That letter made me so angry because so many of the problems they talk about in the letter are still going on. The signatories are all people who I admire and participate in the community. Why are we still having these fights?

Isabel: Yeah, that letter, it brought up all the anger from being on the concom with that one person who so fought the POC-only space. And the worst part is that this person thinks they're being progressive by not wanting to "ghettoize" us.

Julia: Oh, it's for our own good. What would we do without white people to tell us POC what to do? The opinions of a white man are always correct. What were we thinking?

Isabel: How many times did I say, "speaking as a POC..."

Joyce: Of course this person knows better than you, this person is white!

Isabel: Actually, I think it's because this person has fought these kinds of fights before (civil rights, feminism, etc.).

Joyce: It's the "I marched in the civil rights movement so I CANNOT POSSIBLY BE RACIST."

Isabel: It was more like, we fought so POC could be included, and now you want us to separate them??? I wanted to give this person a copy of *Why are all the black kids sitting together in the cafeteria?*

Joyce: I love that book so much. Also someone should link him to delux-vivens' blog posts on the civil rights movement, school integration, and the death of many all-black schools.[8]

Isabel: At least everyone else on the concom was on board.

Julia: It also kills me how people with privilege seem incapable of noticing when they're going against what the group they're "helping" has stated they want and that they're the lone voice jamming the cogs.

8 http://delux-vivens.livejournal.com/.

Isabel: Paternalism runs deep.

[note Joyce left the chat at this point]

The GoH for 2010 and Goals

Isabel: So, I couldn't talk about it between the vote and the public announcement, but I was dying about the GoH selection for next year! Isn't it awesome!

Julia I was on a morning panel when someone told me about it. I almost blacked out from joy. I then made the entire room listen to me talk about how awesome Nnedi [Okorafor] and Mary Anne [Mohanraj] are.

Isabel: I am very excited thinking that this might bring in more unicorns! Like, all by themselves, even. Unicorns we don't even know!

Julia: What I want to do for next year is basically celebrate them, and Nisi, during the entire con.

Isabel: How should we celebrate them?

Julia: Throwing confetti everywhere?

Isabel: The hotel liaison will kill us.

Julia: I'm flexible. How about having a trumpet blast play when they enter rooms?

Isabel: Maybe.

Julia: My goals for next year are to encourage more POC attendance (I reserved two rooms for POC to fill), find ways to celebrate Nnedi, Mary Anne, and Nisi both in advance and during WisCon, and not overload myself.

Isabel: My goals are to be more out there with my activism, including things like getting POC on the GoH candidate list for more conventions.

I wanted to add my eternal love and thanks to all the wonderful POC that make this community so amazing to be a part of!

Johanna: I'm so excited about next year's GoHs! I am hoping this leads to an explosion in number of POCs at the con, & lots of awesome panels with POCs on them (both about race and not about race, of course!). And not a lot of fail. I am nervous about the likelihood of fail, though!

Before We Remember

Robin Small-McCarthy

A sweet quietness calms over her
Washes through her
As fatigue sleeps and nuzzles
In the arms of her inward embrace
Like a child at the end of a trying day

Her shoulders relax
Her breath steadies
Into an easy, rhythmic flow
Inhaling
Exhaling

Her tired eyes close
As her third eye opens
And she sees
That we are all God's children
Although some of us have forgotten
And many do not believe

She remembers
She feels that
In spite of aging bodies
Greying hair
Wrinkles
There among
Limber bodies
Dark hair
Smooth, wrinkle-free complexions
She knows that
In spite or light of
The complex rainbows of multiple shades

Multiple hues
We are all but tiny children
Tots in need of a long afternoon nap

In need of Someone to show us
The beauty of the sun
As it sets at the end of the day
Red, orange, and pink strands
In the clouds
In the sky
Blending

She thinks
We are all in need of Someone
To believe in us
To teach us
How to believe in each other
Again
In ourselves
Again

She remembers
That as little children
We did not see
The multiplicity of colors or
Varying shades of skin tones
As we climbed jungle gyms
As we built castles in the sand
As we listened to bedtime or naptime
Stories
Adventures
Fairy tales

As we told each other
Scary stories, urban legends, and myths
While camping out in the back yard
Underneath the moon and the stars

She thinks to herself
I think I understand
This need to divide ourselves
Into false us-versus-them camps
But she does not believe in that
Will not play that game anymore

She asks
When will we all finally learn and
Believe once again
In our Oneness

Until then
She sighs
How sweet
How calming
How comforting it is
To listen together
Quietly to stories
To tales woven by strong women
Whose voices coax us into
Quietness
Deep listening

Feeling the passage of time
She thinks
How beautiful
How relaxing
For now
Together
Before we forget
Again
Before we remember
To divide ourselves
Again
Into artificial categories
Black
White
Brown

Red
Yellow
Old
Young
Healthy
Unhealthy
Insiders
Outsiders
Able-bodied
Disabled

Without false hope
She is listening
Without grasping
She is breathing

She is content
For now
She is glad
For stories

Happy
She is breathing
Freely
She is
Calming

Before we remember

Robin Small-McCarthy is a well-known poet, singer, and performing artist in New York City's underground poetry and music scene. Her writing has been published in the *Journal of Cultural Studies*, *Nomad's Choir*, and *Sound Identities*, and she has just published her first book of poetry, *Love During Wartime* (Cengage). Robin is currently moving to Madison, WI.